VICTORIA'S
SECRETS

THE TOTALLY AMAZING, COMPLETELY
UNAUTHORISED BIOGRAPHY

VIRGINIA
BLACKBURN

JOHN BLAKE

Published by Blake Publishing Ltd,
3 Bramber Court, 2 Bramber Road
London W14 9PB, England

First Published in Paperback in 2001

ISBN 1 903402 82 4

British Library Cataloguing-in-Publication Data:

A catalogue record for this book is available from the
British Library.

Typeset by Mac Style Ltd, Scarborough, N. Yorkshire

Printed and bound in Great Britain by Clays Ltd,
St Ives plc

3 5 7 9 10 8 6 4 2

Papers used by Blake Publishing Limited are natural,
recyclable products made from wood grown in
sustainable forests.
The manufacturing processes conform to the
environmental regulations of the country of origin.

Shhhhh!

Contents

Very many thanks to Geoff Marsh – without whom I could not possibly have written this book – Dennis Rice, Jane Sherwood and above all to Chris Williams, the mostwonderful editor in the diaspora of Fleet Street.

Shh**1**_hh!_

In the Beginning

When Victoria Caroline Adams was born on April 17, 1974, there was nothing in her background to suggest that she would one day become an international superstar and follow that up by marrying the greatest footballer of his generation. Yes, her father Tony had briefly dabbled in music in the 1960s, performing with a band called The Sonics, but then just about everyone dabbled in music back in the Sixties. Anyway, The Sonics was just a tribute band that never made much of an impact on anyone, something Tony had accepted more than a decade before Victoria was born. His talent lay in business, not music, and it was as an entrepreneur that he made his money and his name.

If truth be told, Victoria's background was the type that produces hairdressers or insurance clerks – her mother was both and her sister trained as the former – not driven pop stars intent on global domination. But it was a unique combination of character and circumstance that led Victoria to become what she is today. She was always interested in singing and dancing, talents she began to develop at the age of three, while problems she encountered at school in her teenage years strengthened her resolve and built up her character until she became a woman quite determined to succeed. Poor Victoria had a horrible time with bullies in her teenage years but at the end of the day – to use her favourite expression – it is she who is the massively successful pop star and they who, in all likelihood, are at the check-out counter of the local supermarket. In her darkest hours, Victoria must look on that as quite a consolation.

Victoria doesn't like to admit it, but she really is a genuine Essex girl: she was born in Harlow. When she was still young, her family moved to north London, where her parents, Anthony Adams and Jacqueline Doreen Cannon, were both born and raised – the two had married four years previously. Three years after Victoria was born, her sister Louise appeared, and then in 1979 the family was made complete with the arrival of Victoria's brother Christian. Shortly after that, the Adams family moved to the country: to Goff's Oak in Hertfordshire. Their house, which had originally been an old schoolhouse, was soon the smartest in the village, and, once Tony had done it up, the only one with a swimming pool.

When she was a very young child, Victoria's life was idyllic. Her parents were growing increasingly wealthy: they had set up Gladerealm, an electrical wholesaler, which was becoming a very successful business. The children grew up with lots of pets and took regular holidays. "I've been on holiday every year since I was born, to the Canary Islands and Spain," Victoria once declared.

There was, however, the odd childhood drama, such as the time Victoria accidentally swallowed poison. "It was a really hot day, I was in my Brownie uniform and I'd just got my safety in the home badge," Victoria recalls. "You know when you really need a drink and you don't just sip it, you glug it down without tasting it.

"Well, I saw a mug of liquid on the side and drank the whole thing before I realised it was a cup of pure bleach. Suddenly, I couldn't breathe. I ran out to the garden where my mum was. 'Stop being so rude, I'm talking to the gardener!' she said as I was gasping away. She thought I was joking! Then she realised and the gardener held me up by my feet and shook me up and down to make me throw up, which is actually the worst thing to do, because it just brings the burning sensation back up. Finally mum took me to the hospital and it turned out OK."

Brownies and drama apart, though, Victoria loved more than anything to dance. The passion for performing stems back to her very earliest days. She started learning her trade when she was barely more than a toddler. "I did some shows when I was very young – two or three," she recalls. "When I was about eight I did one where I was dressed up in a bright yellow top hat and tails with sequins all over it, yellow fishnet tights and yellow tap shoes with yellow tap bows, I danced to *If My Friends Could See Me Now*, that Shirley Maclaine song from *Sweet Charity* – and I was Shirley Maclaine." In adult life, Victoria's heroine actually came to be Audrey Hepburn but, as an indication of what was to come, Shirley's song could hardly have been more appropriate.

Victoria first attended the local Goff's Oak Junior, Middle and Infants School, where her passion for performing grew stronger, and where she seized every opportunity to show what she could do. Teachers said she was a lovely little girl who loved appearing in the school's pantomime. "Victoria was always such a pleasant child, very pretty, not at all loud or pushy," says Sue Bailey, one of her former teachers. "She worked hard and came from a lovely family. I can remember her in the leading role of the Pied Piper. She was always in school productions, very keen on drama."

Tony Rowan-Wicks was Victoria's headmaster. He remembers a very shy, unassuming little girl, very different from her outspoken persona today. "She was just a very sweet girl," he says. "We never had any problems with her. She was quiet though, very quiet. But she was always satisfactory academically – never a problem in the classroom. It never even occurred to me that she might go on to be so famous – it doesn't, does it?"

It did occur to some people, though, most notably Emma Comolli, Victoria's closest childhood friend. The two met when they were both aged five, as they lived only a few miles apart in Goff's Oak village, where Victoria's father Tony had by now transformed that derelict schoolhouse into a stunning family home. Victoria and Emma were drawn together because of their mutual love of dance and drama until their friendship ended seven years later – because Emma became a rebellious teenager while

Victoria never wavered from her in-built work ethic and hunger for success. Sometimes stardom can happen by accident, but in Victoria's case that was emphatically not the case.

Emma, who is now training to be a teacher as well as writing her first novel, recalls how Victoria's desire for fame at first amazed and then isolated her from many of her school friends, – something for which poor Victoria was to be bullied about for many years to come. "Victoria was in no doubt at all that she was going to become a famous singer and dancer," says Emma. "In all the time that I knew her she was rehearsing for the day that she would appear on television. I even remember worrying about it. When I was eleven, I looked at her and thought, 'What is Victoria going to do if her dream doesn't come true?'" As it happens her worries were to be unfounded, but it says something for Victoria's ambition and determination that it was making such an impact on her friends even back then.

Victoria's audiences in those days were made up of friends of her parents, who frequently witnessed the young wannabe and her friends dressing up to put on song and dance performances in the back garden of the family home. "Victoria was a brilliant dancer," says Emma. "She had this balletic ability to bend herself into positions which appeared impossible. I remember thinking as a child that she must have been double jointed in every limb."

She also sang and her innate confidence in her own ability inevitably led to her playing all the lead parts in these amateur productions as the Adams' family revelled in the exploits of their gifted daughter. "I remember Victoria and I absolutely adored *Grease* and unless she was feeling generous she always played Olivia Newton John while I was John Travolta," says Emma. "We also loved the television programme *Fame*. Victoria video taped the whole series and learned all the dance routines and songs from watching them."

Victoria's first attempt to become famous came about when the young friends, aged just eight, wrote to a number of TV programmes. "I remember Victoria and me writing to *Jim'll Fix*

It asking if he could fix it for us to meet our favourite pop star Toyah Wilcox, but we didn't hear anything back," Emma says. "Then there was this programme on TV called *Mini Tots* which Victoria and I absolutely loved. They would invite children on to perform as their favourite pop stars and we had this routine worked out where we were the girls from Bucks Fizz." Unfortunately, the programme's producers missed their chance to have a future Spice Girl on their show – something all those producers of *Before They Were Famous* television shows must now seriously regret.

Victoria and her sister Louise would also practise routines together, including a home-made version of the famous Bucks Fizz number from the 1980s, in which the boys in the band tore the skirts off the girls to reveal another, shorter skirt. And, as ever, at home as well as with her friends, there was no doubt as to who was the star. "She used to get all the fancy outfits and I'd get all the boring ones or have to be the man. I wasn't happy about that," says Louise.

But in many ways, Victoria's childhood was normal. She wasn't as close to her siblings as she later became, and there was the usual share of fractiousness and family squabbles. Her appetites were those of the average child: she used to love McDonald's hamburgers and pizzas, which attracted the disproval of Emma's mother. "My mum would never let me go to McDonald's because she said it was disgusting, but when I stayed over at Victoria's, her mum often treated us by taking us off for a McDonald's or a Wendy burger," says Emma. "Then there were the midnight feasts we used to have of pizza and ice cream. Victoria and I were addicted to this sauce called 'Ice Magic' which hardened as soon as you put it on the ice cream."

But even then Victoria stood out, not least because of her unflappable energy. Emma says: "Victoria had the most amazing stamina I have ever seen. I would be flat out after a day of dancing and singing with her while she would just keep on going." This was to prove invaluable in later years: Victoria and her fellow Spice

Girls practised for hour after endless hour as they learned their trade, which required not only discipline but an enormous amount of stamina.

Performing was an all consuming passion. Victoria did not develop an interest in boys until many years later, as Emma explains. "Victoria simply did not have time for boys," she says. "There was one boy we both adored called Robbie Hart whose father drove a black taxi. He went to our junior school and knew we liked him, but he used to shun us. As far as I knew he was the only boy she actually liked. Victoria wanted to make sure nothing got in the way of her becoming famous." She did have the usual teenage crushes, though. "I really fancied Matt Goss from Bros and I was convinced I was going to marry him," she says. (Ironically, the two men who were to put together the Spice Girls also set Bros out on the road to fame.) "I had loads of Bros records and posters."

Even at that early stage, Victoria was ambitious. From the age of eight, she was sent after school and at the weekends to the Jason

Theatre School in Broxbourne, where, as a result of her own pleading, she studied ballet, tap, modern dance, drama, singing, jazz and national dance. She continued at the school until she was 16. She also took part in shows such as *Hello Dolly* and, in one of the various Spice coincidences that littered the girls' lives until they eventually got together, she actually appeared in a show with Emma Bunton when she was still eight.

Victoria's parents, although delighted with their daughter's prowess, were not pushy towards the young star in waiting. "They're not 'stage school' parents at all," says a friend of the family. "They're very down to earth. Quite disarmingly ordinary people really. Tony still works very, very hard and he's always worrying about whether he's looking after his clients for the electrical goods. He's always fretting over the latest order."

Victoria's teachers, though, were sure they had an achiever on their hands. "The very first time I saw her, I knew she was special," says Joy Spriggs, Jason Theatre School's owner. "She performed in a wonderful costume covered in gold sequins. She had natural talent and you just had to watch her." Victoria did so well that she was awarded three of the school's top trophies: the Senior Choreographic Award, the Shakespeare Shield and the Personality Cup. "She lived, ate, slept and drank dancing," Joy said. "I just thought, 'This girl has got something.' She danced instinctively. She was always in the front row – she had an ability to get herself noticed."

By this time, Victoria was becoming set on a stage career in earnest. She spent hours practising her autograph and fantasising about being recognised in public. In this, incidentally, she has a great deal in common with the late Diana, Princess of Wales, who also knew from early on that she wanted a life centre stage. Diana might have come from the aristocracy and Victoria from the nouveau riche, but both were young women absolutely determined to get their way and both have attracted the fascination of media and public alike. One commentator once even went as far as saying that both became famous because of the man they married, although this would seem to be a little inaccurate as far as Victoria is concerned, at least.

During her childhood, Victoria had the most unlikely inspiration: Barry Manilow. "I remember when I was really young," says Victoria, "my mum dragged me to a Barry Manilow concert and, you know, we sat watching in a great big field covered in cowpats – not very glamorous at all – and I said to my mum, 'I'm gonna be up there one day.'" Her mother must have thought this was a typical teenage fantasy – Victoria, however, was absolutely serious.

And it was the rigorous training that they both received at the Jason Theatre School, according to Emma, that proved to be the key to Victoria's success. "I stayed there from eight until 14 and Victoria was there even longer," she says. "The drama classes were divided into groups of eight to ten and the dance classes up to 20. Everybody was watching each other and we all became a bit secretive about what we were doing. I remember going for auditions for things like soap and shampoo commercials and not telling Victoria. She was the same with me and the other children. It was a very competitive environment which I suppose in a way prepared her for what happened later on."

Home life, however, was happy. Despite the odd moments of sibling rivalry, the family became unusually close, and still is. Victoria has in recent years bought her brother and sister a house and various cars, her mother plastic surgery and still sleeps in her old bedroom when she goes home. "I've always been in a family where there's loads of people round the dinner table and the telly's on in the background and there's something else happening over there," she says. "And I want to create the same kind of atmosphere."

Another irony, though, given that she succeeded in a world marked by its appetite for indulgence and excess, is that Victoria's character was much more straight-laced than rock-and-roll. She probably would never have made it had she not had the self-discipline to practise so hard even back then, but rock stars tend to have dissipated youths, not the swotty variety. Nor was Victoria exactly prone to letting her hair down. Although that later saved her from some of the embarrassments her fellow Spices were later to experience, such as Geri's topless modelling shots, it did cause her problems during her school years.

It was also not initially the image the girls wanted to show to their little fans. Back when the Spice Girls first hit the national consciousness, there was a good deal of spin put about concerning their wild behaviour. The problem in Victoria's case was that there wasn't a good deal of wild behaviour to crow about. She gamely flashed in front of a lift full of strangers in a hotel once and submitted to having her knickers thrown out of a taxi cab's window. But the reality lies in her own description of her childhood.

"I never, ever get in trouble," she confesses. "I'm always really good. Even as a child, I was really boring and really good. But I tell you what I did do once: my dad bought a brand new van and we'd just had a brand new wall built. Me and my brother and sister got in the van and I knocked the handbrake off, so it rolled down the drive and smashed the brick wall in. Brand new van, brand new brick wall – my dad went absolutely ballistic. And I blamed it all on my little brother." So there you have the full extent of Victoria Adam's wild behaviour – blaming her brother for a childhood accident. It's rock and roll, Jim, but not as we know it.

All was not, however, sunshine throughout Victoria's childhood. In fact, the really difficult stage was about to begin, partly because of her studies at Jason Theatre School and partly because of jealousy from other girls in the village about her family's wealth. "When we both started going to the Jason Theatre School in Broxbourne, we were the only girls in the village to go," Emma recalls. "Victoria was also the lead in every single production at Goff's Oak Junior School and because of that there was a lot of jealousy. People knew her Mum and Dad lived in the biggest house in the village and Victoria used to be dropped off in the morning in the family Rolls-Royce. She absolutely loved being driven around in it like a little princess.

"People also knew that her family owned a villa in Spain, which they used to go off to every summer. And although a lot of the other children we knew at the time came from well-off families they used to pick on her. It only happened in a very small way at Goff's Oak and nothing prepared either of us for the reception we got at St Mary's School in Cheshunt. I had become a bit of a tomboy by then and used to go out to the park with the boys on my BMX while Victoria wanted to keep practising her singing and dancing – so we grew apart."

This was doubly unfortunate as, looking back, Victoria could have benefited from some moral support from her friend. At the age of 11, she started secondary school at St Mary's, Cheshunt in 1985, which proved to be a miserable experience. She was constantly bullied at school until she left five years later.

Every topic was considered fair game: her ski
jump nose, her acne (Victoria suffered badly as
a child and to this day won't leave the house
without heavy make-up to conceal the scars),
her father's wealth, her goody-goody nature and
her preference for taking dancing and singing
lessons after school rather than following the
more usual teenage pursuits of smoking,
drinking and snogging. "Victoria had a bad time
at senior school," says her sister Louise. "People
didn't like her because she didn't go out every
night and hang around street corners, instead
she used to go to a lot of singing and dancing
lessons."

Neither were fellow pupils impressed by the
fact that she was delivered to school in her
father's Rolls-Royce – after a time she used to
beg her father to drive her to school in his van.
The taunts began: her schoolmates took to
calling her Goody-Two-Shoes and Acne Face.
Teachers would have to escort her to the school
gates and that waiting Roller. "The other kids
used to tease her because sometimes her dad
would drop her off at the school gates in his

Rolls-Royce even though she lived just round the corner," said one.

It was a horrible time for many of the pupils at the school. "I only found out much later that she was being bullied by the same girls at St Mary's that I was," says Emma. "They used to trample on your blazer and do things like throw your pencil case down the stairs. It sounds comical now, but it was really scary then. I used to skip school because of it, but Victoria would come in everyday and hand her homework in on time. She hated the bullying and basically just got through it.

"Her Dad would drop her off in the Rolls-Royce and her Mum would sometimes wait at the gates with little presents for doing well in things like the spelling tests. Victoria always worked hard when there was an incentive. She was very good at maths but less so at English so her mum would set her a 20 word spelling test once a week. If she got 20 out of 20 – and believe me she would make sure she would – her mum would give her a pair of hot pants or some Pineapple dance clothing. She even got this beautiful green catsuit for getting a spelling test right once."

This, however, was small consolation from the bullying. Matters were made worse by Victoria's aloofness and her family's wealth. "She used to turn up in a really smart car while all the others went by bus," says Emma. "After school her dad would wait for her in his gold-coloured Rolls-Royce. Nobody liked this very much. Victoria always dressed very smartly and never mixed with any of the others. Some were very jealous of the money her family had. Her mum was very proud of Victoria and would tell everyone how wonderful she was. This irritated people."

And, unwisely, Victoria chose to highlight the differences between herself and her fellow pupils. "Victoria would talk about how rich they were and how she wanted to be famous one day," says Emma. "So the others would turn on her and call her names. I once watched her getting pushed around after school by the gang. They used to pick on others as well, me included. They called themselves "The Mafia" and everyone was scared of them. Once they even put a girl in hospital."

Victoria's experience with the bullies was clearly traumatic. She has in adult life frequently referred to the bullying that made school such a misery, as well as highlighting good causes designed to put an end to bullying in schools today. "I was one of the most unpopular kids there," she says. "I was a complete wreck. I would wake up worrying who I was going to sit next to in class. It was sheer hell." And on another occasion she remarked: "I know myself that children can be awfully cruel sometimes. When I was growing up I was the victim of some really nasty bullying at school."

Nor was Victoria the fashion icon she was later to become. "I wasn't a stunning teenager," she says. "I was bullied at school because I had bad skin, so I wasn't confident about the way I looked back then. I was also picked on because I was just different to the other kids. At the time, all I wanted was work really hard and do my best, but that wasn't deemed cool by the rest of my class. It was really, really hard for me and I never had any real friends at school. It was a horrible period of my life, but I had my family to support me – my parents were so upset whenever I came home crying. My heart goes out to anyone who is bullied, because children can be so cruel, physically and mentally. I get a lot of letters from fans saying they are bullied and my heart breaks reading them. I wish I could do more to help."

Victoria, however, was always concerned about her looks, even if she wasn't pleased with them. "I've always been bothered by my appearance," she says. "I used to wear make-up to school and as soon as I got in I'd be told to wash it off. And I didn't do PE because I thought it would mess up my hair. My mum used to write and say I'd been injured. That's probably why I've been labelled the way I have."

Paradoxically, however, that bullying might well have given Victoria the determination to succeed that would stand her in good stead several years on. It is a well known fact that high achievers tend to come from unhappy backgrounds and despite the closeness and warmth of her family, there is no doubt about the fact that Victoria had a truly awful time at school. There are two ways to deal with this: to go under or to survive. To sink or to swim. And, to quote the late Princess Diana, with whom Victoria has so much in common: "I swam."

This urge to say "I'll show them" could certainly explain why Victoria has succeeded in the way she has for, as she herself is the first to admit, there are many more talented performers out there who haven't had a smidgen of her success. She's average looking, an average singer and an average dancer and yet through sheer force of willpower, she's turned herself into a glamorous star.

In this she again resembles Princess Diana, who turned herself from a plump Sloane Ranger into an international beauty concerned with humanitarian causes. And while comparing Victoria to female icons of the late twentieth century, there's another she bears a certain resemblance to as well, namely

Madonna. Madge also started out as a dancer, is also not the greatest singer of the age and also displayed steely determination right from the word go to make it to the top. When she was first starting out, like Victoria, she had no time for really close friendships and even at this stage in her career, like Victoria, she has unfulfilled ambitions to be taken seriously as a movie star.

No one would be more pleased than Victoria to invite comparisons with Princess Diana and Madonna, but there was little sign of what lay in the future when she was in her teens. "I was picked on a lot at school," she says. "I was never particularly good at anything at school, but I had a lot of drive and ambition. I didn't even have a nickname because nobody would talk to me." That last recollection is in direct contradiction to her known nicknames, but the message stays the same: I showed you eventually. I won and you didn't. Oh, and I do have a nickname now: it's Posh.

The young Victoria did, though, have a normal childhood in some respects and, like most little girls, was fascinated by clothes and make-up. She was actually about 13 when she first started wearing make-up: "It was bright blue eyeliner and I thought I was really cool." Her obsession with make-up remains to this day. Victoria always wears some, and lots of it. In one of her first major interviews after the Spice Girls had hit the big time, an interviewer comments on how much make-up Victoria is wearing for such a young woman, not least because she remains self conscious about the scars from when she had acne.

And, goody goody she might have been, but Victoria was beginning to find out about adult life, not least when she started going to night-clubs from about the age of 14. "Not very credible clubs I might add," says Victoria, "tacky ones, in fact. I had a good relationship with my mum and dad. They never minded picking me up at three or four in the morning."

They were very harmless places as well, and very different from the nightclubs in London and Ibiza that Victoria was to sing in when she was promoting her first single. As an introduction to the clubbing scene, they were ideal though and a far better preparation for being a member of a group than, for example, hosting a Turkish television game show, as Geri Halliwell did.

The clubs were also ideal for developing her own dress sense and style. Victoria remembers what she used to wear and it was a long way from the Gucci and Prada that were to become her favourite labels. When she was with the Spice Girls she once remarked that she hadn't made any really bad errors in the fashion sense. Asked if she had ever had a real fashion disaster, she said, "No, I've been lucky. I'm quite good at knowing what suits me, but sometimes I look back at old photos and think, 'Oh, that skirt was so short the whole world could probably see my knickers. But I don't count that as a disaster. The mini-skirts I wore when the Spice Girls came out were kind of what made me. Everyone dislikes outfits from their past, but it's never a disaster if you thought it looked great at the time."

That wasn't entirely the case back in her teens, as Victoria is the first to admit. "I had hot pants, which I wore out clubbing," she says. "I also had a big, terrible perm. I thought people were looking at me because I was so cool, but they were probably thinking, 'What a mug!'"

Shhhh!
2

Waiting in
the Wings

The torture and the bullying that was
Victoria's lot at school did, however, finally
come to an end – for a while. At 16, with a
reasonable set of exam grades and more
focused than ever on what she wanted to do,
Victoria applied for and took a three year
course at the Laine Theatre Arts College in
Epsom, Surrey, one of only 200 pupils to be
accepted in 1990.

Founded in 1974, the school is one of the
leading performing arts centres in the country,
teaching all aspects of musical theatre and

dance, with other alumni including Lee Latchford-Evans of Steps, Katie Bradbury and Lisa Kay from *Hollyoaks* and Kerry Ellis, who recently made her name as Martine McCutcheon's stand-in in *My Fair Lady*. Victoria worked hard, stayed ambitious – and remained realistic.

"It wasn't easy because I wouldn't say that I have natural talent," she declares. "I wasn't the best and I was never picked for auditions. I worked hard but it was a struggle. Some of the teachers used to say to me, 'You'll never make it' or 'You don't look right.' It was because I didn't have long legs, blonde hair and natural acting ability. But there were others who encouraged me." It was also at around this time that Victoria started to become aware of her weight. By normal standards, she wasn't fat at all, but in the world of show business, where to strive to become rich, you will almost certainly need to be thin, she was acutely aware of the need to become sylphlike. Victoria is 5'6" tall and at the time weighed about nine and a half stone, which is perfectly normal for her height. However, Victoria was not content with her body and this was to become a problem as she got older. She now says that it was Geri's obsession with dieting when she joined the Spice Girls that tipped her over the edge, but her entirely false self-perception that she was too fat dates back a long way.

Worries about her weight aside, though, her determination was beginning to pay off. Victoria's ability to admit she's not the most talented singer and dancer in the world actually paid off, for she simply realised that in order to succeed, she was going to really have to work at it. And work she did. This determination paid off: she might not have been the first to be picked for auditions, but she got a couple of assignments: some modelling jobs and dancing at the celebrations for the Rugby World Cup. She has never lost that ability to work for what she wants: the Spice Girls famously spent 18 months rehearsing before they were ready to take on the world. Even now Victoria puts in the hours, whether it is practising dance routines or conducting publicity tours around the country, her workload would stop a lesser mortal in his or her tracks.

However, just as she had done at school, Victoria was beginning to have problems with some of her fellow students. Victoria's character could be a curious mixture of aloofness and arrogance, and that combination could come across as seemingly very cold. She was a boarder at the school initially, but again that clean-cut manner let her down and she found her fellow students constantly bitching about her behind her back. It was an improvement on school, but not much and Victoria wanted to move out.

For the first time, however, Victoria had something in her life other than family and focused ambition: a boyfriend. She had not been very interested in boys when she was growing up – apart from the odd crush on the likes of Luke from Bros and a very short term experience when she was young. "When I was 13 I had one of those silly boyfriends – you know, the type you only go out with for two weeks?" she says. "I only went out with him because he kept pestering me to, but I got bored and finished with him and he cried." Even then Victoria would treat them mean and keep them keen.

Victoria, however, was nearly an adult now and was ready to start forming relationships with the opposite sex. The lucky man who became Victoria's first boyfriend was called Mark Wood: Victoria had met him when she was 16. He was a security consultant – or to put it another way, he installed burglar alarms – who lived nearby and who had done some work for her parents, which is how the two first encountered one another.

He was her first serious boyfriend and first lover because, somehow inevitably, Victoria was too sensible to sleep around when she was a teenager, and anyway, she didn't want to. "I wouldn't have sex on the first date," she declared in an interview before she got married. "I know I wouldn't be able to cope, because I'd get too emotionally involved. Some people feel embarrassed if they haven't slept with many people, but I don't think it matters.

"When I was younger, people tried to pressurise me into sex and I wouldn't do it. I've always been a strong personality and if I don't want to do something, no one can make me do it. Too many people think that because all their friends are doing it, they should, too. But everybody should make their minds up about it." It is ironic in the context of this that Victoria was criticised when she became pregnant with Brooklyn before she and David married – a more sensible piece of advice to Victoria's army of young fans would be difficult to imagine.

Victoria finally did make her mind up about Mark: seven months after the relationship began, according to Mark himself, after Victoria had consulted her mother about the wisdom of the move. And to begin with, certainly, the relationship was based on love. When the couple first met at her parents' house, Mark was 19 and so instantly smitten that he finished with his girlfriend of a year's standing in the hope that Victoria would go out with him. He then started turning up at the house on any pretence. "I ended up going round there just to check everything was OK with the alarm," he says. "It was really silly. Sometimes I didn't even see Toria. She had left school but was always at dance classes. And I later found out that sometimes she was there but didn't want to see me because she wasn't dressed up.

"I thought she was gorgeous. She was a cute and giggly kind of girl and quite shy. I eventually phoned up and asked her out. It was one of her first ever dates and she was really nervous. She asked for a Bacardi and Coke and by the time I had paid, she had drunk it all. She knocked them back and by the end of the night she just sat opposite me, smiling and giggling. She was so shy and not at all the confident pop star you see on TV now. She even thought she was fat and ugly because she had a few spots." This is a rare example of Victoria drinking, incidentally. While not exactly teetotal, the only excess in her life is around her workload. And it is telling that even then she was paranoid about her appearance.

Some months after the relationship began, Victoria went off to Laine's where, again, she was found it difficult to get on with some of her fellow pupils. This time, however, she had a boyfriend as well as her family to lean on, and Mark went on to provide a great deal of moral support in those early, difficult days.

Just a couple of days after she started at the school, she rang Mark in tears. "Toria said she was too fat," he says. "She had put on a few pounds after going on the Pill. She said the other girls were awful and she wanted to come home. Sometimes she would ring in tears every hour but I would persuade her to stay and tell her how much I loved her." And this really did highlight Victoria's odd mix of assured ambition and vulnerability: she could be devastated by an unkind remark but, underneath it all, never lost the conviction that she was going to be a world famous pop star.

Matters eventually improved: Tony bought his daughter a two-bedroom flat in her second year. Victoria shared it with four other students, which would have been good practise for when the Spice Girls set up house together briefly in Woking and then in Maidenhead. Nor was she as isolated as she had been at school. There were also some other would-be dancers around, with whom she got on well and made friends with, in as much as Victoria is capable of making friends.

Tamsin Sessions was one of them, and remembers yet another example of Victoria's unshakeable conviction that she would succeed. "I remember my mum sitting next to Vicky's mother at an open evening and Jackie telling her that her daughter was going to be a pop star," she says. "Vicky had not mentioned this to me and I was a little taken aback when I heard her mother had said that. We were all about 18 then and most of us had absolutely no idea what we were going to do."

The friends kept in touch with each other for some years, right up until Victoria told Tamsin that she had joined an all-girl band which was sharing a house together in Woking. She spoke of her doubts as to whether it would work. "I guess this was before they moved into the house they eventually shared in Maidenhead," says Tamsin. "Victoria told me she wasn't convinced it was going to take off and she was looking around for a 'back-up' just in case. She was very driven even then." And she certainly believed in keeping her options open, refusing to make a total commitment neither to a band nor to a man until she was absolutely certain she had found the right one.

Part of that drive emerged when Victoria arranged to have a set of photographs taken of herself and Mark. For the photographer in charge this turned out to be anything but a normal photo shoot. It was not the easiest of jobs for Geoff Marchant, the photographer who helped many of the students at Laine's prepare their drama and dance portfolios, and gave some indication of what was one day to come. For a start, Victoria had to be persuaded to smile (to this day, that remains the case) and, unusually for one so young and inexperienced, she wanted to dictate camera angles and pictures, rather than leaving it to him. That, incidentally, is one more thing she has in common with the late Princess Diana: during the famous Panorama interview, it was Diana who called the photographic shots rather than the programme's producers.

In this series of pictures published in this book, which have only recently come to light, Victoria sets the agenda: it is she who decides on the poses she strikes and the way each shot is positioned. She poses, she pouts, she practises for the future. It is an astonishing performance full of poise and self assurance, from a young woman who could have had no idea how famous she would eventually become.

Geoff has photographed hundreds of young women who have gone on to become household names but remembers Victoria standing out – not only because she refused to smile very often, but also because she had such a clear idea about how everything should be done. "She came to see me twice. Once with another dance student and on another occasion with her boyfriend

Mark to have some photographs taken of them together." he says.

"Usually students trust my expertise in the business, but Victoria had very strong ideas of her own. She wanted a sort of moody look and told me straightaway what lighting and camera angles to take. She also refused to smile at first but I eventually succeeded in getting her to relax a little on that. I had to contact her about where to send the pictures so I asked her where she was living. She told me that her father had bought her a flat in Epsom. That was unusual in itself because most of the students at Laine's shared digs. I think Victoria made up for that by getting a few of the girls in to share her flat."

You can see why the other Spice Girls, who all came from more working-class backgrounds, thought she was Posh. Despite still being a teenager, Victoria was quite grownup. She had her own flat and she had also got her first car. Victoria has always loved cars. In addition to driving around in a series of flashy numbers of her own, she has given cars to David, her parents and her siblings in the years since she has become rich and famous.

The relationship with Mark seemed a happy one. Mark tells of holidays at the Adams' holiday home in Riviera del Sol in southern Spain, and romantic dinners cooked by "Toria" herself. She would send him love notes. On his twenty second birthday, Mark received one saying: "I'll still love you even when you're old! Lots of love from your little pop star! Victoria, xxx." Another Valentine's card reads: "Mark, I know this is meant to be a secret, but I guess you know already who this is from! Anyway, it's no secret how I feel about you, even though we have our ups and downs. I'll love you forever. Victoria, xxxxx."

The relationship seemed to be going from strength to strength. Mark moved into the Adams's Hertfordshire home shortly after Victoria returned from Laine's. "I moved in with Toria after she'd had an argument with my mum," he says. (This was not the only time Victoria has had run-ins with her men folks' parents. Much later rumours were to circulate that there were tensions between Victoria and David Beckham's parents. It is also no secret that she has an extremely strained relationship with Sir Alex Ferguson, who might be called David's surrogate father.) "She was so happy, she wanted to have me all to herself and was used to getting her own way," says Mark. And, as we know, what Victoria wants, Victoria gets. Mark moved in.

At that stage Victoria wasn't getting her own way in every sphere of life, though: she'd passed all her exams at Laine's but life was by no means easy. She entered the audition circuit, enduring countless rejections along the way, which she both took to heart, blaming her weight and acne, and rose above, determined that she would become a pop star. Another Spice coincidence happened at this stage (remember, she had bumped Emma very fleetingly when they were children): she met Geri for the first time when they both auditioned for (and didn't get) parts in the film *Tank Girl*. But there was the odd job, and she finally landed a part as a chorus line dancer in a

Birmingham production called *Bertie*. Victoria was on her way.

That job was a much-needed ego boost, even for one who was so certain that she would succeed as Victoria. On hearing the news, she tore home to her parents and Mark. "She flung her arms round me and started screaming," Mark recalls. "She'd been for loads of auditions and this first job was just the confidence boost she'd needed." Joy, however, was followed by a pang, as the couple realised they would have to spend long periods apart and so Victoria did the sensible thing – she proposed.

"I didn't say yes right away because I knew my parents wouldn't be happy," says Mark. "But, at the same time, deep down, I knew Toria was the one for me." And so the preparations for the engagement began: after failing to find a ring in Hatton Gardens, the diamond centre of London, Mark paid £1,500 to have a ring designed and made himself. (David Beckham's engagement ring for Victoria was worth £40,000.) Victoria even began to call herself Victoria Adams Wood, a name that can still be seen on early Spice Girls merchandise and the name by which she introduces herself in *Raw Spice*, the television documentary that was made about the early days of the Spice Girls.

And the young couple played it by the book. Mark very properly asked Tony for permission to wed his daughter: the Adams parents were delighted that their daughter was to settle down. "I was dreading asking him but he was thrilled and he picked Toria up in his arms and gave her a huge hug," says Mark. "Her mum organised a huge engagement party straight away." Mark then took Victoria for a special celebration dinner: half way through he got down on one knee and placed the ring up on her finger. "She looked beautiful in a long, slim fitting red dress," he recalls rather wistfully. "We ordered a table at a restaurant beside Tower Bridge. Her mum had flowers and champagne sent for us. It was a beautiful and romantic evening. Toria was the sweetest girl I had ever met and I wanted her to be my wife."

But Victoria was also the most ambitious and driven girl he had ever met and in reality, she was not yet ready to be anyone's wife. Even as her mother was arranging the engagement party, with guests sipping champagne beside the swimming pool in the parental home of Goff's Oak, Victoria had not forgotten her career and she was determined to sort that out before she got married. Her time with *Bertie* had come to an end and it was back on the audition trail, with nothing much coming up. She was determined to be a pop star. It was just a matter of time before the right opportunity came along.

Still, these rejections were hard to deal with and, as usual, Victoria blamed her imagined physical defects. "She still thought she was fat and ugly," says Mark. "Her mum used to call her Cruella de Vil – she still does. But Toria was always beautiful with a lovely figure. She had a small gap between her teeth which she hated. She said smiling made her look ugly, so she had it fixed." Victoria really does have an obsession with that smile – even after dealing with her teeth, she still didn't like to smile because she thought it made her look as if she had fat cheeks. When the Spice Girls got together, this false impression intensified after she saw early publicity snaps which, in retrospect, make it clear that Victoria has a perfectly nice smile. But, alas, she doesn't like her dimples.

As it happens, Victoria's next break was actually not that long in coming. After another audition, she was accepted into a band called Persuasion and she stayed with them for six months, meeting up to rehearse a couple of times a week. She was never fully committed to them, however. Perhaps sensing that something bigger was in the offing, Victoria continued to attend auditions for other bands. One of these was for an all girl band and after auditioning for that, she was accepted, which, as we shall see in the next chapter, turned out to be the biggest break in her career. But we're getting ahead of ourselves. The rise and rise of the Spice Girls is a story in itself – for now, at least, Victoria was weighing up the various avenues open to her and deciding which would be the best one to pick. As the world now knows, she made the right choice.

Perhaps inevitably, Victoria's relationship with Mark was not to last. Until now pop stardom had just been a dream, even if it was one that Victoria was prepared to work very hard for. But now, it seemed, there was at least a chance that dream would become a reality. Victoria was a member of two bands and was coming under pressure from the fellow wannabes in her newest group – the girls – to choose between her career and her man. At that stage, young, ambitious and hungry to make it, there could never be any real dilemma as to which she was to choose.

Victoria stayed with Mark for a time after meeting the girls, but the strains were beginning to tell. There were increasing numbers of arguments about trivial matters. They nearly split up over an argument about a pair of sandals Mark had bought for Victoria – she wanted to wear them straight away, he wanted her to wait until her birthday – but they eventually reached a compromise. (This is also an indication of the fact that it is not a good idea to argue with Victoria about clothes: clothes are dear to her heart and she will not countenance anyone trying to ration her access to them. After their first date, David Beckham gave Victoria a handbag. The gesture impressed her enormously and did nothing to prejudice her view of him.)

The strain continued to grow, however, and after five and a half years together – by this time she was completely committed to this new band, who would soon turn into the Spice Girls – Victoria told Mark it was over. The poor boy cried himself to sleep for three weeks but to no avail: "She said I was pathetic and should get on with my life, because she was," says Mark. "She was going places and didn't need me any more." It was a fairly brutal way to treat someone with whom she had spent half a decade, but Victoria clearly felt it was the right way to handle the situation. She once said that if you are horrible to an ex boyfriend, it makes it easier for them as they can then go off and hate you. It is not absolutely certain that that strategy worked in Mark's case. Some people believe he holds a candle for her to this day.

There was slightly more to it than the fact that Victoria no longer needed him, though, as Mark discovered some time later when Victoria left some pictures lying around. Most uncharacteristically, Victoria had behaved like a wild living rock chick, and had a fling with the actor Corey Haim, star of *The Lost Boys*. The couple had met in 1995 when Corey was in London, cutting a demo tape for Polygram. The engineer at the West London studio in which the American was based was dating a certain Geri Halliwell. One day the other members of Geri's band trooped into the studio to meet her handsome beau, and Corey set eyes on Victoria, who was in the early stages of turning herself into Posh Spice. In the best Hollywood tradition, he announced, "I have got to have that girl."

The Hollywood heartthrob was successful. He began chatting to the team, who were, it seemed, a little in awe of his star status, before persuading Victoria to show him the sights of London. This she did with commendable enthusiasm, touring him around everything from Buckingham Palace ("the castle where your Queen lives," according to Corey) to the Ritz Hotel, where the two engaged in a full-on fling. This being Victoria, however, the relationship almost immediately became respectable, with Corey being taken on tours of the English countryside – and home to meet her parents.

The two were by all accounts inseparable, but it really was just a week long fling. "I had a great time," says Corey. "I totally know Victoria and I also got to see a lot of the beautiful English countryside. She always made sure I was OK. Victoria is really intelligent and she was cool to hang out with. But as I live in the US and she lives in England, there was no future for us." And so he went back to the United States and Victoria continued to turn into a Spice Girl.

It was shortly after this episode that Victoria ended the relationship with Mark, although she didn't mention Corey to him then. It was only an unfortunate slip that revealed the truth. "They had a week-long thing. He was staying at The Ritz and she stayed with him until he returned to America," says Mark with a touch of understandable bitterness. "She left pictures of him and her on the kitchen top. They had their arms around each other and looked very happy."

The bitterness lingers and there is little love lost between Victoria and Mark's families now. "She [Victoria] said some really nasty things about him in the press, especially after he told his side of the story, but he never responded," says Joan Wood, Mark's mother. (Actually, Mark sold a kiss and tell story about Victoria, as we will see later on in the book.) "He's never been nasty back to her even though he's had plenty of opportunities – he just isn't like that. He was always there for her, caring for her. All the way through her college years he was absolutely devoted to her. What thanks does he get for that? None at all, just abuse." This doesn't worry Victoria. She is married to David Beckham now, and the early days of dating Mark Wood must seem as if they belong in another life.

It does seem to have taken Mark a long time to get over Victoria, though. In 2000 he appeared on Blind Date and spent pretty much his entire date in Tenerife reminiscing about his ex, a tactic which didn't go down too well with his chosen partner, Julie Gibbs. "I didn't have the heart to tell him to shut up," says Julie. "I get the idea he's still infatuated with her. In fact, he looks like a male version of Posh Spice. I think they would be ideally suited."

Even on the first night of the holiday, Mark couldn't keep his feelings for Victoria under control, talking for two solid hours about his ex. "As soon as we met he began talking about her," says Julie. "I think he was playing on it a bit. On the first night he went on about how they met and the early days of the Spice Girls, about how he got on with her parents and family and how she got on with his. And wherever he went, he would be saying Victoria this, Victoria that. It got quite tiring after a while.

"I did get the impression she wasn't as lovey-dovey with him as she is with David Beckham. He said she was very domineering and liked to be in control as well as being a bit of a bossy boots. At one point he actually said he felt sorry for Beckham because of her nagging and sometimes he thinks he's better off without her, but other times he misses her."

Joan Wood is scathing about Julie's account of the date. "He went on [the show] because he thought it would be a bit of a laugh. But it was just a slap in the face," she says. "As soon as he was paired with that girl, he said to her, 'I know they've made a thing about Posh Spice, but it's all in the past. I'm living my life now, not several years ago.' They never even talked about her on their date. But as soon as they got back she was mouthing off to the press and on television saying about how 'Posh Spice ruined my blind date' and how Mark was still obsessed with her. It was all just nonsense."

As for Mark himself, his own words reveal a couple who were fundamentally mismatched. On the eve of her wedding, sitting in the one-bedroom £43,000 Hertford flat that he had bought for the two of them, he commented, "If I had married her, our kid would probably be called Bournemouth or Blackpool, not Brooklyn. They travel the world, yesterday I went to Rotherham on business. All she ever wanted was to be famous, but she also has the man to go with it." And at this juncture he disclosed that his car, a five year old Jeep, is worth less than £10,000, which is a far cry indeed from David Beckham's garage full of sports cars.

Victoria was equally breezy about her first serious relationship. "It's no secret that I've been engaged before, but I had no intention of getting married," she said brightly, on the eve of her wedding to David. "It was just the thing to do at the time. But then you meet the right person. As soon as I met David, I thought, I want to marry this person, grow old with this person, learn things about life with this person … have a family. I surprised myself. When I met David, I thought, yes, I do really want to get married."

So it probably wouldn't have worked out with Mark, and Victoria did finally get her ideal man. However, Girl Power or no, she also did what every erstwhile fiancée worth her salt does. She kept the ring.

Shh*3*hh!

Wannabe

We want to be a household name. We want to be a Fairy Liquid or an Ajax. Victoria Adams

It was an innocuous enough advertisement by anyone's standards.

R U 18–23 with the ability to sing/dance?
R U streetwise, ambitious, outgoing and
determined?

The year was 1993 and the ad had been placed in *The Stage* by, of all things, an accountant. Bob Herbert, who sadly was killed in a car crash in 1999, was a showbusiness actuary from Lightwater, Surrey and together with his son Chris had already created one famous pop group – Bros. Luke Goss, one of the twins who made up Bros, had been dating Herbert's daughter Nicky and, sensing the boys had talent, he had allowed them to rehearse in his summer house. He even roped in his elderly aunt Ethel, a talented musician, to play keyboards with them and the work paid off. They made it, but only after their relationship with Bob had run its course.

It was a good learning experience for both Bros and Bob, though, and noting the success in the early Nineties of boy bands such as Take That, New Kids On The Block and East 17, Bob had a brilliant but simple idea: create a girl band. Find five women in their late teens and early twenties with differing but complementary looks, personalities and back grounds, mix them all together and what have you got? A pop sensation.

That is exactly what happened, of course, but it wasn't quite as simple as that. It was also very carefully thought out. First the father and son team created a "mood board," a chart of all the personalities they wanted in the band. They then set out to find them, first in West End clubs and pubs and then through auditions. They were also determined that there should be five girls in the band. "It's a very complicated formula," said Bob in an interview shortly before his death. "We wanted five personalities that would actually bond together. And we wanted five because if you have four kids, they're always arguing, two versus two. With five, there's majority rule."

Bob and Chris linked up with Chic Murphey, a self-made businessman who had not only been a secondhand car salesman in his time, but had also once managed the Three Degrees. Just like Bob did with Bros, Chic got the American trio going, but lost contact once the group had become famous. His dream was to run another famous group: this time with five women rather than three.

First auditions were held in a studio in South London on March 4, 1994. Four hundred girls turned up: each was given 30 seconds to sing and given marks out of 10 for singing, dancing, looks and personality. Victoria made it through, despite a derogatory remark on the original records about her skin. A shortlist of 11 was drawn up and then, two months later, a twelfth name was added: Geri Halliwell. The final auditions were to be held in Nomis Studios, a low, inconspicuous-looking building in Shepherds Bush. It was surrounded with residential housing, and net curtains hung in the studio's windows.

Victoria felt a rush of excitement combined with nerves as she entered the studio. Recognising Geri from the *Tank Girl*, audition, she smiled at her before being called up to a low stage, where Bob and Chris were seated. "Bob looked like an extra from Miami Vice," recalls Geri in her autobiography. "He had a sun tan, wore a white suit, pale-blue shirt and brogues. He had gold rings on his fingers and looked like he was in his late forties. [Bob was actually nearly 60.] His son, Chris, was long and lean, with a Timberland shirt hanging out of his jeans and his hair slicked back. I think he quite fancied himself."

Each girl was asked to talk about herself and they were then divided into two groups of six girls each. Each group was given a song –*Just A Step From Heaven* by Eternal – and told to go off and work out a dance routine, which they were to perform half an hour later. From there, the numbers were whittled down to five, one of whom was another newcomer, Melanie Chisholm, who had missed the audition because of tonsillitis. The five girls – Victoria, Geri, Mel C, Melanie Brown and Michelle Stephenson – were then called back for another tryout and finally sent to a guesthouse in Surrey for a week to see if they got on together. They did.

Victoria was different from the others. She had finally met people with whom she had a great deal in common – drive and ambition – and so it isn't surprising that she made some genuine friends at last. She had more money than the others, though, and her own car, which meant that she could go home at weekends. "Her parents had a bit more to spend," said Bob. "Her parents were successful business people. So she had nice clothes."

It was at that guesthouse that preparations first began to mould the girls into their hugely successful personas. Despite having had professional training, none of the girls was anywhere near the standard required for even a modestly successful outfit, let alone the phenomenon that the Spice Girls would one day become. They weren't even called the Spice Girls at that stage – the first name for the band was Touch. That the name had five letters was deliberate, incidentally – one for each member of the group.

Victoria, however, had one minor problem: she was already a member of another band. In fact, she had been in Persuasion for the best part of a year (and given how dire everyone said she was when she joined the Spice Girls, it is perhaps fair to assume that even if that band had stayed together, they would never have made it. That, however, we will never know.) Now 18 years old, Victoria had to choose between her old band and her new one and with that ruthless streak that propelled her to the top, there was no question about what she was going to do. She chose to do out with the old and in with the new. She also did it just as her old band was on the verge of their big break.

Her fellow band members – Persuasion, that is – were, unsurprisingly, appalled. Steven Andrews, who had put the band together, couldn't believe what Victoria had done. "We were all devastated when she quit," he says. "We couldn't believe what she had done to us. It felt like we had been kicked in the teeth. I had always wanted to form a band and saved all my life to make it work. I advertised in August 1993 and had hundreds of applications. But as soon as I saw Victoria's picture, I knew I had to offer her a place.

"She looked so sexy in the photo. She was dressed all in black with a pair of sunglasses on. It was just the image I was looking for. Her CV said she had been to drama school but hadn't sung professionally. I didn't care. I wanted to see her in the flesh. My feeling was right. She walked into the room and looked great. She was a shy mummy's girl, but that was half the attraction. She wasn't a great singer but she had potential and I knew I had found the right girl. She was hungry for fame and willing to work hard."

So were the other members of Persuasion. As with the Spice Girls there were five, but it was a mixed group comprising Steven, Victoria, Steve Monday, Natasha McLauchlin and Nathalie Watkins. Funnily enough, Victoria appeared to be the worst in the group. "Everybody pulled together," says Steve. "The only problem we had was Victoria. She froze when she had to sing with a microphone."

At that point Victoria was still with Mark Wood, who would insist on turning up to watch practise sessions, which took place twice a week. "She was never late or moody," says Steven. "She just got on with it. She sometimes got upset about Mark because he was so possessive. He used to sit in at rehearsals, which I hated."

If truth be told, those twice weekly sessions bear no comparison with the non-stop gruelling routine the Spice Girls were to put themselves through before they became famous. They also gave Victoria plenty of time to attend other auditions and, indeed, to start working with the girls as she had been doing since May of that year. Nevertheless, there was some interest in the band. In order to drum up interest from record companies, Steven arranged a launch party at the Discotheque Royale in Uxbridge on August 28, 1994 and some representatives of independent labels agreed to attend.

"It was our big chance to become famous," says Steven. "Victoria kept checking that she was doing everything right. She was really nervous because she was singing the lead in a ballad. I brought a solicitor in and was about to get everyone on contract to show that we meant business. Our dreams had really started to take shape. It had taken a lot of work, but we were ready."

And then came the bombshell. With less than two weeks to go before the big day, Victoria had to make her choice and here her ruthless nature came into play. She had been flitting between the girls and Persuasion for some months now and it was becoming increasingly obvious where her future lay. The

Herberts wanted the girls to move in together and so Victoria finally had to own up – and leave. "I remember it like it was yesterday," says Steven. "She had been to the Spice Girls audition behind my back. I couldn't take it in. She knew damn well that we couldn't replace her before the launch. I was so angry I couldn't speak. I kept asking her how she could do it to all of us and she kept apologising."

Then Steven had to break the news to the other members of the band – and everyone else. "I had to cancel the night," he says. "It was horrible. I lost all credibility. People were shocked." Nor did the band survive. "I returned to modelling for a while," says Steven. "Steve Monday did a Nurofen advert and the girls were unemployed. It was really sad." But Victoria Adams, soon to be Posh Spice, was on her way to the top.

The Herberts owned a management company first called Heart and then Safe, and it was through this company that they were training the girls. They were under no illusions about the work to be done, and were well aware of Victoria and the other girls' singing and dancing deficiencies. So they got in touch with Irwin Keiles, a musician who had worked with the father and son duo on their Bros project.

When the girls first became famous, they angered Keiles and quite a few other people by their claims that they had done it all by themselves. The story at the time was that the same five girls kept bumping into one another at auditions, failing to make the grade, bumping into one another at the next audition, failing to get called back until, exasperated by their lack of success, they decided to make a go of things together and – hey presto! – the show was on the road. This disingenuous tale may have got them in the newspapers, but it is not what happened.

"It is complete rubbish," says Keiles. "A lot of hard work by other people prepared them. Bob and Chris were very clever. They knew exactly what image they wanted and were very specific about the girls they were looking for."

One of those other people, and one of the most important people to feature in the early

Shhhhh!

days of the Spice Girls was Pepi Lemer. Pepi is a well known voice trainer and she was hired by Irwin with one instruction: make them stars. This was easier said than done. Hours, days, weeks, months and years would be required to do that and, back in the middle of 1994, it didn't look promising. "The first time I saw them was in a studio in Surrey," says Pepi. The studio in question was Trinity Studios, a run down dance school that had seen better days.

"They'd had to learn this song that Irwin had written called 'Take Me Away.' I remember them being quite attractive in their different ways, but terribly nervous. They were shaking and when they sang, their voices were wobbling. It has to be said that they weren't very good. My first impression was, 'There's a lot of work to be done here.'" Funded by Chic, the initial plan was to have a long session once a week with the girls, but it soon became obvious it was going to take a lot more than that. Pepi ended up taking them through twice weekly four hour sessions for the next nine months.

There was also the living accommodation. Chic had a three-bedroom house that was empty in Boyne Hill Road, Maidenhead and so the girls moved in: Victoria and Michelle shared one room, the Melanies another and Geri, as the oldest, got one all to herself. "It was a shoebox," she says. The girls were each given a £60 a week allowance to cover basic living expenses, which they supplemented by signing on. The stage was set.

And it was not, initially, easy going. Pepi remembers constant tears and tantrums from the girls as they began: "There were quite a few times when I really had to gee them up," she says. "They didn't really want to have to go through all this, it was damned hard work. One might have a headache, the other would start crying, another would run out of the room and the remainder would start arguing."

Pepi would frequently have to hug the girls as they burst into tears and remembers sitting at the piano playing a single note, which the girls would have to sing over and over again. "No, that's not the note," she would say. "Sing it

again. Sing it again." And still there was no
indication as to what was to come. "I remember
looking at these incredibly ambitious faces and
saying to them, 'It's like a lottery, girls. If you
make it you will be very lucky'," she says. They
did make it and they were very lucky, but in
fairness all of them had prepared themselves for
what was to come, not least Victoria. She knew
she had to become a good singer and dancer, and
she worked hard to become one.

Another person who played a crucial role in
their success was Ian Lee. Ian ran Trinity Studios
in Woking and, like Pepi, helped to train their
voices. He met them in that first week and he,
too, scoffs at the early stories put about by the
girls. "I couldn't believe it when all these stories
came out about how the girls did everything
themselves," he says. "They were a put-together
band. They'd never met until they were picked
from 400 others and Emma Bunton and Geri
Halliwell weren't even considered for the
original line-up. They couldn't sing and they
weren't the greatest dancers, but they had one
thing in common and that was blind ambition.

They spent a year working like slaves to get things right and once they got things sorted, they dropped everyone and took themselves off."

Ian worked with the girls for the best part of a year. Like Pepi, he would sit at a piano with them and help to train their voices, but was not impressed when they all first met. "They sounded absolutely awful," he says. "Geri had problems singing in tune and none of them could move together. After a few days you could see something gelling but it was no overnight miracle. It was bloody hard work."

After the girls moved to Maidenhead, Chris Herbert paid Ian £100 a week to allow them to use his studio. "They lived quite simply," says Ian. "They'd eat lunch at the local tea shop or bring in sandwiches. They usually wore the same clothes every day." Apart from Victoria, that is, who paid attention to her wardrobe even then.

Ian watched the girls as their relationships with each other developed and the dynamics of the group began to form. "Geri and Melanie

Brown were instantly singled out as leaders," he says. "They always had an opinion and they both wanted to be in the driving seat. They used to fight like cat and dog. Geri would stand there with her arms by her sides and her fists clenched as Mel would have a go at her for singing out of tune. Melanie Chisholm would always act the peacemaker and the other girls would just watch in stunned silence.

"Geri would freely admit she wasn't a great singer or dancer, but she was a damned hard worker. She's spend hours on her own perfecting her singing or working on her dance steps. She was determined to succeed. She kept running around saying, 'Time's running out. This is my last chance and I'm going to make it.' She was a tough nut. She always had a vivid imagination, and she'd expect people to believe her, whatever."

Not that it was all work and no play. Mark Brownsmith, who was then Mel B's boyfriend, recalls some riotous times. On one occasion the girls dressed up as St Trinian's schoolgirls, and would often turn up to local parties. "Every weekend there were noisy parties at the house next door and the girls always made an appearance," he says. "They used to dash in, run around squealing and flirting and trying to make all the boys fancy them and then race back to their place. They were always making a lot of noise."

Well, most of them were, anyway. Victoria was still seeing her Mark and, as attached to her family as ever, often went home at the weekends. But she was as ambitious as the rest of them: "The girls were always saying they were going to become famous," says Mark. "They told us: 'Take That are finished – this time next year we'll be them." As it happens, it took a little longer than a year – but in time they well and truly overshadowed Take That.

For the moment, though, a new problem was looming: Michelle Stephenson. Michelle had never really fitted in with the other girls and was increasingly regretting her decision to join the group – even though she had been the first to be chosen. Formerly a member of the Young Vic and National Youth Theatre, Michelle had seen the advertisement in The Stage while studying English and theatre at Goldsmith's University in London and went to the auditions to gain experience. To her own surprise, she made it through to the finals and, as she had just completed her first year at university, spent the holidays with her four new friends.

She remembers those days with a certain amount of fondness. "Victoria was addicted to cornflakes with honey – she'd eat them at any time of the day," says Michelle. "She got me hooked on them, too." And she recalls how the girls began to develop their nicknames. "Victoria was the posh one because of the way she dressed – she had some beautiful clothes," she says. "The idea was that each of us would appeal to a slightly different fan, something they stuck to when they became the Spice Girls – and it obviously worked."

It didn't work for Michelle, though, who had set her heart on becoming an actress. Two months after moving into the house, the Herberts had to tell her it was not working out and she left by mutual arrangement. Michelle however, has never regretted what happened: after leaving she travelled around Europe before returning to Goldsmiths to complete her degree. "Of course I regret I'm not a multi-millionaire like them," she says. "But at the time I left the group I knew I was doing the right thing, and I still think it was the right thing. It wasn't my kind of music and they were not living the lifestyle I wanted."

"She wasn't like the rest of the girls," says Ian Lee. "She was quite reserved and pensive and wouldn't always agree to do the things the rest of them wanted. The girls used to moan about her and it was obvious that something was going to have to be done. Then her mum got cancer and she ended up quitting the band."

Michelle's departure, of course, provided an opening in the group that was filled by Emma Bunton, who had been taught by Pepi some years before. "Chris held a panic audition and Emma was picked," says Ian. "She was far more suited to the rest of the girls, although she would go on about how much she missed her mum." Emma fitted in much better than

Michelle had done. "Emma went down to meet the rest of the girls in the house, and the next time I saw them she seemed to have integrated perfectly," says Pepi. "She did miss her mum, though. It was a bone of contention between the girls. At weekends, both Emma and Victoria would go home and Geri would get annoyed as she wanted to practise." According to Ian: "Melanie Chisholm, who is the real talent in the band," (or was, if rumours she's left are true) "would spend all her spare time watching football. Melanie Brown and Geri were the ones who'd do all the partying. And even though they'd do most of the fighting, they were the ones who'd go off together."

Pepi also found a new role in her relationship with the group: that of social mentor. Victoria has been widely teased for not actually being all that posh, but she was the epitome of sophistication compared to the rest. "One evening I cooked them dinner," says Pepi. "One of them poked at the smoked salmon, wrinkled up her nose and asked me why it wasn't cooked. They were incredibly naïve and sweet."

It was during this period that the band started to become the Spice Girls, although the origin of the name is not entirely clear. One of their neighbours at the time was Mabel Brobyn, a pensioner. Mabel had a little Lakeland Terrier called Spice and has always wondered if the group's name originated there: "Occasionally, the girls came over to ask my husband for help," she recalls. "One time, they'd locked themselves out and he lent them a ladder. Spice was always around and we'd constantly be calling out his name. I'm sure that's where they got it."

Ian Lee tells a different story. "They got their name from Tim Hawes, who co-wrote a song with them called *Sugar and Spice*," he says. "They were sitting around afterwards and he said: 'There's your name. It's perfect because you're a bunch of spicy bints.' They loved it."

It was also during this period that the girls made a decision that they came to regret. Geri had a friend called Matthew Bowers, who was a researcher for the BBC. Matthew mentioned this group in the making to his friend Neil Davies, a former paratrooper who had become a film maker and, with the full consent of the girls, decided to make a documentary about the group's progress. "The girls were up for it," says Neil. "They knew any publicity would help them on the road to the pop star world."

And so filming began. Viewing it now, it is hard to see why the girls objected so much when it finally came to light early in 2001, because, while nothing like the polished act they were to become, their enthusiasm and good natures do shine through. Victoria is caught on camera confessing to a crush on Ryan Giggs (what his fellow team mate David Beckham thought of this has never been revealed) while Geri says of her, "I think she's the older man's kind of date. She adds sex appeal to the group."

Victoria also admits to sucking her thumb and reveals a battered old stuffed rabbit, which is not what always first comes to mind when you think of rock and roll. And there are also premonitions of what is to come – Geri and Mel B are seen arguing furiously, while Mel C laments, "I feel like I'm losing my identity. I wake up with this scary feeling that I don't know who I am." But the girls come across as they were – young, a little naïve, very enthusiastic and extremely ambitious.

And it gave Neil himself a chance to observe the girls at close hand. "We met them in rehearsals," he says. "They were all really nice, bubbly and full of life. They were just having a good time, but were absolutely convinced they were going to be pop stars. The driving forces were always Geri and Mel B – they were the leaders of the gang. There was a very powerful creative tension between them. Geri most of all was absolutely desperate to make it. Mel C was very pleasant – more concerned about others than herself – she was just a nice girl. Emma and Victoria were a bit shy, but they opened up in the gang atmosphere, because that is fundamentally what it was – a gang."

It was also a very disciplined gang. "It was like a boot camp," says Neil. "They were running every morning, doing exercises and then on to singing practise. They were sacrificing everything.

When you saw them like that, you really wanted it to happen for them."

Certainly the documentary portrayed them in a fresh, new light. Victoria was undeniably plumper than she has been in recent years and a little more versed in the social arts than her friends, not least because she was the only one who shut the door when she went to the loo. She also declined bathside chats with her fellow Spices. "I love this bath," Mel B is seen as saying. "You can guarantee that when you're in it, someone will sit and talk to you – except Victoria." "Just because I wear clothes when I walk around the house and shut the door when I have a wee," explains the posh one herself.

When the documentary finally hit the TV schedules, the girls threatened to go to court. The reason is a mystery, but perhaps the girls were alarmed when the programme was finally aired on ITV in March 2001 under the title "Raw Spice" because they had simply forgotten about its existence. By a bizarre turn of events, the film went missing for years, having failed to find a television slot when it was first touted

around in 1995. Neil put it aside, thought no
more of it, and decided to return to it at a later
date. But in 1996, when he was on holiday,
thieves broke into his studio, ransacked the
place and left with all the equipment and film
footage they could find, including that of the
Spice Girls.

Neil himself tracked the missing equipment
and material down and a long legal battle
ensued. He eventually demanded to see some of
the film in their possession, and to his own
enormous surprise, found it was the missing
footage. This time round, the television
companies were only too happy to bid for it –
only for the girls to threaten legal action.
However, Neil did actually have the paperwork
in which they agreed to be filmed and so the
world finally got to see them in all their early
Spicey glory. The story did have one very sad
note, though – Matthew did not live to see the
documentary screened. He died of bowel cancer
in 1997, at the dreadfully early age of 27.

Back in 1994 all this excitement and drama
lay ahead. Now, with nearly a year's solid

training under their belts, the girls began to feel it was time to show the world just what they were made of. Irwin Keiles and his partner John Thirkell wrote five songs for the girls and Pepi set up a showcase in a studio in Earl's Court. The aim was to find the group an agent.

"The girls had written this rap thing to go in the middle of one of the songs, which we really liked," says Irwin. "Unfortunately, they'd changed the lyrics and they were appalling – they didn't rhyme or fit in. But by then they'd become quite brazen and when we told them we'd revamp the lyrics they didn't want us to."

There is some controversy over what happened next. The girls were clearly becoming unhappy with Chic Murphy and the Herberts – and vice versa – and wanted to leave. By this time it was early 1995 and the official Spice line is this: they had never signed a formal contract with Safe and were now finding the men too controlling and too demanding. Geri has since said that when the girls were finally given contracts, the Herberts demanded 25 per cent. In response to this, the girls ganged up together and left.

That is certainly the way that Ian tells it. "By that stage, they'd become really good," he says. "Chris was a great artistic director and he'd got them working so all their weaknesses were hidden. The way they look, sing and dance together is exactly the way he got them to, even down to the way they stand. He was the one who got Mel Chisholm to do her acrobatics as part of the act. He wanted them to be sassy and sexy, which they were. You could see they were going to make it. And they started to act like real pop stars."

In Ian's version of the story, their departure was sudden and dramatic. It was April, 1995. "The last time I saw them, they were working in the studio, when suddenly there was this massive row between the girls," he recalls. "The whole building could hear them screaming and shouting at each other and then they all burst out of the room and stormed off." That was the last Ian saw of them. "Afterwards, I even wondered whether the whole thing was staged," he says.

"Perhaps they wanted us to tell the Herberts that they'd split. Still, they disappeared and the next thing was that we read in the music press was that they were signed up by Annie Lennox's manager, Simon Fuller, and had done a deal with Virgin. I was really pleased when they got to Number One and I tried to get them to do something for Trinity, and support the charity organisation which is here to help young artists get on their feet. But I was blanked by their management.

"All Emma ever wanted was to be on the cover of *Smash Hits* and the rest of them wanted to be on *Top of the Pops*. They've done all that and good on them. They worked hard and they deserve it. It just seems that the business has made them hard enough to brush aside their past and make out none of us existed. Considering all we went through together, that is such a shame."

This story is borne out by the Herberts. "The girls just went," said Bob. "They left the house and that was it. I have no idea where they slept that night." The girls had been due to go to a songwriting session with the composer Elliott Kennedy the next day, so Bob rang Kennedy's manager to cancel. "The man was baffled, 'What's going on?' he said. 'They're here.'" There was nothing the Herberts could do: the girls wanted out and they got out.

Pepi felt similarly snubbed by the girls when they went on to find fame and success. "When the girls moved on, they sent me a card which said: 'Thank you for everything, we could not have done it without you,'" she says. "So why won't they now give credit where it's due? I said to myself when I turned on the television, 'Did I do that?'"

All good, heartless stuff on behalf of the girls, but there is another version of the story, a much less Girl-Powered version: that they were sold as a group to the man who was to become their manager, Simon Fuller. "It was a direct hand-over to Simon Fuller," says one person who claims to have been involved in the transaction. "Mutual agreement was reached." A figure of £50,000 has been mentioned.

This is also born out by a source close to the Herberts. "The girls said they'd pay back what they owed and sort it out amicably," he says.

"Then they went to see Simon Fuller and he became their manager." Whatever the truth, however, given that the girls abruptly dropped the likes of Pepi and Ian and went on to dump Fuller in the course of time, it seems there is one nickname that would have fitted the lot of them. Ruthless Spice.

Shhhhh!
4

Zigazig Ha

Simon Fuller is an unlikely Svengali for one of the noisiest, one of the brashest and one of the most successful bands in pop history. "Modest to the point of invisibility", according to friends, Simon, a short, chubby, raven-haired figure with a year-round tandoori tan, and his company 19 Management were already well established figures on the music scene when the Spice Girls hurtled into his orbit.

But Simon was exactly what the girls needed. He had drive and ambition to match their own, he knew the music scene inside out and, most importantly, he knew a good thing when he saw it. And the Spice Girls were a very, very good thing.

Simon's childhood contains hints as to what was his future career would be. Born in Cyprus to an RAF pilot turned teacher, and brought up in Germany and Africa, Simon and his family eventually returned to England to settle in Hastings, where he was sent to school.

Showbiz was, however, already in the family, in the form of a grandfather who was a music hall comic and acrobat. And Simon's entrepreneurial talents didn't take long to come out. While still at school, he offered to manage a band called Billy Whizz, which was made up of some schoolmates. "Really, we were all playacting at being in bands, but Simon seemed very serious about it," says Andrew Smith, a member of Billy Whizz. "His parents gave us the basement of their house to rehearse in and he hired out Hastings Caves, which no one had done before, and put us on there. He promoted it heavily within the school and turned it in to a big event. It was packed and Simon actually made a lot of money."

And it seems that Fuller harboured no illusions when it came to where his talent lay.

The other boys dreamed of being rock stars – Simon dreamed of being a rock star's manager. He knew that he was good at making money and that the creative part – the writing and singing – could come from elsewhere. "He made one attempt at songwriting," says Andrew Smith. "We were struggling with a lyric for one of our awful songs and he said, 'Boys, I've got one for you.' And he'd written this atrocious thing about 'a shady lady in a negligee.' I don't think we ever let him forget it. In fact, we used to take the mickey out of him mercilessly because we considered him to be gauche."

On this point they were very wrong. Simon wasn't just ahead of his pack when it came to the serious business of making money, he also trumped them in the amorous stakes, as well. None of his contemporaries could understand why. "He had no sense of irony," recalls Smith, "which as a teenage boy is your stock in trade. The funny thing about Simon is that we always thought he was quite effete. He had this very middle class accent and a big moon face – rather like a young Paul McCartney – but he always, without fail, went out with the most beautiful woman around. We couldn't understand it. We thought we were it but we couldn't get the girls, so I asked Simon what his secret was and he said, 'I just go up to them and ask them out.' And that was it. We'd never have asked but Simon would." This was an attitude that was to take him to the top of his profession in the years to come.

On leaving school, Simon decided not to go to university, against his father's wishes. Instead, he started running local discos. "It was completely against anything Dad believed in," says Simon, "but he was forgiving. I was lucky in that. The thing about Dad was that he was an entrepreneur at heart. He was proud that whenever he bought a car, he sold it at a profit. Even now I feel like I'm doing what he might have wanted to do." His next big step up came in 1983, when he became a talent scout for Chrysalis Records.

Simon clearly had a nose for what he was doing. He proved his worth almost immediately by signing up *Holiday*, which became Madonna's first hit in 1984. "I remember him bringing in Madonna's *Holiday*," says Terri Hall, who worked for five years with Simon. "And this was when she was completely unknown. Simon had been offered the song and the artist for $10,000 and he was pushing very hard for Chysalis Records to take it. Chrysalis said, 'Pick the song up but don't bother with her, she ain't going nowhere.'"

A year later, in 1985, Simon decided to go it alone. "After two years I was earning very good money. And I thought, right I've done that," Simon recalls. "It's tragic how easily I wanted to go off to the next thing." It was, however, the next thing which made both his name and his fortune. Taking Terri with him, Simon left Chrysalis Records in May 1985 to become Paul Hardcastle's manager, and he did not have long to wait before discovering he'd made the right move: two weeks later Paul hit number one with the song *19*. It didn't quite achieve the success of *Wannabe*, but it was not far off: it sold four million copies, hit the number one slot in a total of 14 countries and made "a couple of million pounds" for Simon. In acknowledgement of this, Simon's management company, telephone number, house number and car license plates all carry the number 19, and the men remain friends and work together to this day. "I steer clear of managers, but I had complete trust in him," says Paul. "He would never rip anyone off."

Terri recalls the frenzy that took place as Paul's record sold 65,000 copies a day. "It was mental," she says. "We were in the office every night until 11, exhausted, but even then Simon would be saying, 'In five years, I see us as more of an umbrella company with a publishing arm, and we'll do films and manage bands and do our own merchandising.' It wasn't because he had a huge ego and wanted to build an empire, it was just what he was going to do. I've never met someone with so much drive and vision. He always said, 'Ambition is not a virtue,' but he ate, slept and breathed his work." And his vision came to pass, as well, when he finally linked up with the Spice Girls, who did not only music, but also movies and merchandising. But that was yet to come.

With Paul Hardcastle proving to be such a success, Simon went on to build up his repertoire of artists. At first, he had only one act other than Paul: a band called The Adventures. Although they never really became famous, he still managed to negotiate three record contracts for them. "He was incredible with contracts," says Terri. "Almost subversive." And again he proved adept at spotting up-and-coming stars who had been ignored elsewhere: against the advice of industry insiders, he next signed up Cathy Dennis, who released 10 singles that made it into the British Top 40.

Perhaps his greatest pre-Spice coup, however, came in 1990. The Eurythmics had just split up and Annie Lennox was looking for a new direction. Fuller acted fast and, promising to make her into a truly global star, wooed and won the Scottish singer. "It seemed like the most obvious outcome in the world to Simon," says a source close to Annie. "Although the track record for artists leaving dissolved bands and going on to become big solo acts wasn't great, he couldn't see how Annie could fail." He was absolutely right, as well: Annie went on to become an even bigger star in her own right than she had been when working with Dave Stewart and ended up as one of the wealthiest women on the British music scene.

Quite apart from his drive, talent and ambition there seems to be an aspect to Simon's personality that appealed to Annie and later to the Spice Girls. In a world driven by ego, Simon Fuller appears to be a genuinely nice man. By all accounts, he is not given to screaming matches, treats everyone courteously and does not, on the surface at least, appear aggressive. "Simon is extremely light-hearted," says Terri. "He's about as far from that banging your fist on the table type manager as you can get. He's very polite, he won't shout and scream, but he gets what he wants by being thoughtful and studied. If there's a problem, he goes away and thinks about it and comes back with a solution. He's also very playful, very joking. There'd be times when you think, 'Can't he just be serious for a moment?' That sounds contradictory for someone who has achieved so much, but that's just what he's like."

Even so, you don't succeed in the music business without some hard-nosed streak in your character. Not everyone is so fulsome in their praise for Fuller, not least because he appears to be one of those people who tells you what you want to hear and then goes off and does exactly what he wants, regardless. "Simon has a unique ability to frustrate and confound," says one person who worked with him and doesn't want to be named. Another associate calls him a "nightmare, and a short, dyed-hair, fake-tan nightmare at that."

Nightmare he may have been to some people, but for five girls hungry for fame, he was Saviour Spice. His conversation with Terri in 1985 practically set out what he was going to do with the girls, not only manage the band, but make a movie and sign countless sponsorship deals. And, with a solid reputation behind him and so much experience in the business, he was the perfect choice for the girls.

As with so much of Spice history, there are conflicting accounts as to how the girls met their man. In her autobiography "If Only," Geri

Halliwell says that the girls first heard of him from friends of theirs, the men who ran a production company called Absolute, and that these men passed on a demo tape that the girls had made to Simon. Simon then made that crucial call. The other version – and this is the one music industry insiders go for – is that the girls placed an advertisement for a manager, Simon called and that was it.

Either way, it was Simon who got in touch first, a decision he was not to regret. The girls walked into his office in Rampton's Dock, Fulham, and it appears to have been love at first sight. That softly softly approach hit the spot. In her autobiography, Geri recalls him saying, "I think you're fabulous. With or without me, you girls are going to make it. But if you tell me where you want to go, I will try to take you there. You tell me to stop and I'll stop." And how could five hungry girls resist a chat up line like that? They had been begging the Herberts for some time to be allowed to record a single, but the Herberts, feeling cautious, held back. Here was a man, though, who believed in them and wanted to show off their talents to the world. There was no question about where – and with whom – they wanted to be.

Simon was equally smitten. "I thought, shit, I know there's something here, I know I can get them good songwriters and good songs," he says. "But how the hell do you market a girl group? And I consciously, methodically, did my homework for weeks. I thought, OK, girls buy girl magazines, they go and see girl movies, they hang out together. But with music they buy boys. I worked out that girl groups had invariably been sexy and that this threatened girls with the thought that they might take away their boyfriends. So the Spice Girls had to be different. Girls have got to identify with them, so they can't be threatening. And everything they do has got to be marketed on those lines."

It was a perfect example of Simon's ability to go away and think out the solution to a problem. He also added the final touch to their name: "When they came to me they were called Spice and I added the 'Girls,'" he says simply. And although it was not so much Girl Power as

Brain Power, given that they had now been together for 18 months, the girls were now a highly polished and professional team of troupers. They were absolutely ready to take on the world. They simply needed someone who knew the business to offer a guiding hand.

And that Simon Fuller most definitely did. Those 18 months in Maidenhead have been written off by some industry insiders as a time in which the girls failed to make it, but the truth is that they were learning their trade. Their singing and dancing, although by no means at genius level, was slick and entertaining, and they knew one another properly now. They knew how to act on stage together, they knew how to cover for one another's faults and boost one another's strengths, and they were capable of adapting to each other – a talent that proved invaluable after Geri left.

Simon saw this and set about making the girls his own. First he had to deal with the Herberts, settling contractual details and almost certainly reimbursing them financially (probably for £50,000). The Herberts had to all intents and purposes supported the girls for the previous 18 months, remember.

Now it was time for Simon to put his own individual mark on the band. For a start, it was he who thought up the Spice Girl nicknames – Ginger, Sporty, Baby, Scary and, of course, Posh – and it was he who encouraged the girls to dress and act in each individual persona. He continued to encourage Mel C, aka Sporty to incorporate her acrobatics in to the act and he taught the girls how to hide their weaknesses. Under his management, a real buzz was beginning to surround the group.

The future was looking increasingly bright for Victoria and the girls and she was happy in her personal life, too. Shortly after splitting from Mark, she met and fell in love with Stuart Bilton. Stuart, now 28, had already had a couple of celebrity girlfriends: he had dated two EastEnder stars, Patsy Palmer and Danniella Westbrook, before linking up with Victoria in 1995. In more recent years, he's dated Martine McCutcheon and Bill Wyman's ex wife Mandy Smith. He could have had no idea back then that Victoria was about to overshadow them all: she was just a girl who lived locally and wanted to be in a pop group. Stuart lived fairly close to her parents, next door to his father's florist and skip hire firm. Unemployed at the time, Stuart would help his mother out in the flower shop. He and Victoria met in a local bar, where they were introduced by her younger brother Christian.

From the time when she was 16 years old and started going out with Mark Wood, Victoria has never spent more than a couple of days, weeks at most, as a single woman. She clearly likes the security of being in a relationship and Stuart came along at just the right time. Victoria was living at home again and at first, the couple seemed to be passionately in love. When Victoria was away, Stuart would drive around in her £18,000 purple MGF convertible, which came not from rock star spoils but her family, and, like Mark before him, Stuart spent an enormous amount of time with her parents. Unlike Mark, though, he didn't actually move in. Neither did they ever get engaged, although friends were sure they would at the time.

It's not that surprising that they didn't, however. Victoria already had one broken engagement under her belt, and would have been cautious about notching up another. Her life was changing fast and it might be that this time round, she was beginning to wonder if she wanted to be hitched to a local boy. Stuart was handsome and good company, but he was not a famous actor, he wasn't even a famous footballer. He was simply someone who was nice to have around. But would it be forever? Probably not.

Victoria herself certainly didn't seem to think so. Now under the tutelage of Simon Fuller, who encouraged her to pout provocatively, flirt and tease outrageously with the other girls, Victoria later confessed, "I never tell anyone I have a boyfriend, just in case there's a better offer around the corner." There was, of course, but he was off training with Manchester United and their meeting was still a couple of years hence.

Stuart's lack of finances can't have helped, either. Victoria's family might not have been posh but it was wealthy and Victoria was looking for something similar. "I hate paying on a date," she said some years before she met Beckham. "I want someone to pay for me. I like being treated like a lady. Ambition turns me on. A man who knows what he wants and goes and gets it. I'm attracted to men with a lot of control and success, real go-getters. Success is always a turn on." And on another occasion, she was asked about her favourite chat up line. "It thrills me when a man comes up to me and says, 'Wanna go shopping on my credit card?'," she said chirpily. "That'll do nicely." Looking back, poor Stuart didn't stand a chance.

Virgin Records, though, did. Simon Fuller had not been wasting his time, and had encouraged the girls to work with Eliot C Kennedy, who was co-writing songs with Gary Barlow of Take That. The girls also met the songwriters Richard Stannard and Matt Rowe who helped the fivesome to write *Wannabe*, the almost ludicrously catchy single that was to be their first number one.

Wannabe was also their manifesto to the world. For a start it sets out their credo: "If you wanna be my lover, you gotta get with my friends, Friendship lasts forever, friendship never ends." Secondly, it describes each one: and Victoria is, as sung by Geri, "Easy V, she doesn't come for free." It was the perfect introduction to the girls and the perfect showcase for their talents: when the video came out, we see Geri and Mel B leading us into the song, Mel C back-flips down a long table, Baby looking demure and Victoria pouting and posing at the rest of them.

The next step was a record contract. By this time, quite a few companies were expressing an interest in the girls and the band ended up with a £500,000 deal with Virgin Records: good money and good terms. They agreed that Virgin would provide the marketing, but that Simon and the girls would always have the final say. This proved a very good move when it came to releasing their first single, but not so good as far as the record company was concerned, when the girls began promoting other products. That, however, was still more than a year away.

The girls were thrilled as they saw that their dreams really were finally about to come true.

"Suddenly we had record companies and publishers queuing to sign us," recalls Geri. The day we signed with Virgin, I wanted to stand at the top of Big Ben and shout, 'We're going to be famous, did you hear that, FLIPPIN' FAMOUS!'

"We signed the contracts and as the champagne corks popped, we were each handed a cheque for £10,000." The girls also handled the situation with a certain amount of panache. On the day the deal was signed, July 13, 1995, a stretch limo drew up alongside the waiting executives, the door was opened – and five inflatable dolls popped out. The bemused record executives took a moment to realise it was a joke: the girls themselves arrived a few minutes later.

The group then went off with Fuller to celebrate: he took them to dinner in an elegant restaurant in West London called Kensington Place. That evening provided Victoria with one of her few reckless, rock-star moments. Unused to drinking very much, after a couple of glasses of champagne, she was completely smashed. The girls had to prop her up until they got her

in to a cab, where they managed to get her
knickers off. Geri promptly threw the prize out
of the window, to the chagrin of the cab driver
and the hilarity of everyone else.

And Simon, with his years of experience in
the business, knew the importance of winning
friends and influencing people: even before
their first single was released, the famous five
went on a promotional tour around the world,
meeting influential figures in the media. It was
essential to create and maintain that all-
important buzz. In Los Angeles, they even
dressed in red bathing suits to pose as Baywatch
babes.

The home territory was tended to, as well. In
February 1996, with contracts signed and songs
recorded but five months to go before their first
single was released, the girls' record company
took their new band to the Brit Awards, where
they caused a certain stir. People at adjoining
tables were curious as to the identity of the
intriguing looking gang of girls – who are they?
Should we know them? were the questions
passing through everyone's mind.

It was, incidentally, one of the more memorable Brit Awards: Michael Jackson performed a song and provoked absolute outrage when he finished his number and adopted a Christ like stance, surrounded by children, as he ascended to Heaven. Jarvis Cocker expressed the sentiments of many of the audience when he ran on to the stage and waggled his bottom at the eccentric singer: Jackson was unaware of the gesture (or at least said he was) and it was edited out of the television highlights, but it greatly entertained those present.

Geri recalls the night, and the curiosity they aroused, in her autobiography. "I spied Nikki Chapman, our PR lady, sitting at a table with Take That," she wrote. "I went up to say hello to her, but avoided looking at the boys in case I was caught staring. I kept thinking of all those nights we spent dancing around the living room in Maidenhead singing Take That songs. I was too old to be one of their fans. A bit later, I went to Nikki's table again, this time with the girls. Jason Orange said, 'Hey Geri! You all right then?'"

The girls could hardly believe that they were on the receiving end of such attention, and all this, mind you, before a record had even been released. If *Wannabe* and its follow up turned out to be a flop, an awful lot of people were going to end up looking very stupid. Clearly, the band could not be allowed to fail.

Nor did it look as if they were going to. Breakthrough followed breakthrough. Initially teen magazines were reluctant to feature the fab five for exactly the reason Simon had predicted: "Our female readers always hated all-girl bands," says one former teen magazine editor. "They fear they will steal their boy idols." When they turned up unannounced at one teen magazine to schmooze with the staff and publicise their soon to be released debut single, the editor couldn't be bothered to leave his office to meet with them.

But gradually, as the Girl Power message started to sink in, those editors saw that this was a girl band with a difference. They actually put friendship before their boyfriends, as their philosophy explained in *Wannabe*. This was very important for pre-teen girls, the target audience, who might have a crush on a boy, but whose actual relationships were far more likely to involve the girls they played with as friends. No opportunity was missed to explain the philosophy of Girl Power, although no one was absolutely sure what it was – something which seemed to involve combining feminism with lipstick, perhaps. "Feminism was you wore crap clothes and let your underarm hair grow," explained Victoria at the time. "We're saying now you can wear short skirts, but that doesn't mean you're gonna be dominated by a man." The girls were also keen to emphasise the strength of their own friendship and by that stage it was almost certainly true: you don't spend a year and a half living, eating, sleeping and sharing your dreams in the close company of four other women without forming some kind of a bond.

The girls also realised the potential that lay in being role models for the pre-teens as opposed to taking on their slightly older siblings who wanted to be cool and were thus more likely to be fans of Oasis. "We are telling children, if you wanna be an astronaut, be an astronaut, you go for it," said Victoria. "When I was at school, I said I wanted to be a singer and a dancer and everybody said to me, seriously, do you want to work in a bank or a shop? And – no disrespect to those jobs – but if kids have a bit of ambition, why let that be knocked out of them?" Why indeed?

The girls were also canny enough to know that their girl next door looks would also appeal to their fan base. "We are also saying you don't have to be skinny and six foot tall and have no spots and be beautiful," said Victoria, whose teenage acne still played on her mind. "We are normal girls."

That they were not. Normal girls do not put in the amount of time and effort that it takes to become a Spice Girl. Normal girls do not have the drive and dedication of Victoria Beckham, *née* Adams. Normal girls do not have, in the words of Richard E. Grant's character in *SpiceWorld: The Movie*, a schedule rather than a life. Normal girls do not grow up to become incredibly famous pop stars who marry incredibly famous footballers. Normal girls, rather, went and bought the records of the Spice Girls because somehow the Spice Girls made them feel that if the Spice Girls could do it, then anyone else can do it, too. Normal girls are far more likely to be found in the banks and shops that Victoria didn't want to work in, but just like the Spice Girls, normal girls dreamed of being superstars.

That is how the Spice Girls hit the big time. Little girls related to them and so, after a fashion, did bigger ones. And, after all, there was something for everyone with the Spice Girls: the glamorous one (Victoria), the mouthy one (Mel B), the tomboy (Mel C), the sex kitten (Geri) and the girl next door (Emma). And that was before you even took their nicknames in to account. They were appealing in a naïve way in those early days, as well, giving every impression of being as excited as their audience about the adventure on which they had embarked.

And then there was the girls' unerring ability to spot the moment for a publicity stunt. The first live rendition of *Wannabe* was not in a concert hall: remarkably enough, it was an impromptu gig at Kempton Park racecourse. In the wake of the Brit Awards triumph, the girls had been invited for a day out by their new record company and, spilling out of the corporate tent, they spotted a bronze statue of Red Rum. As one, the girls rushed over, clambered on to the horse's back and let rip, before the security guards got them back down on the ground. It was possibly this one act that finally guaranteed, if further guarantee were needed, the record's success: their antics had been spotted by Vincent Monsey, the chief executive of the pop cable TV channel The Box.

"When I saw the Spice Girls on top of Red Rum, their personalities came right through and I knew they would do something big," says Monsey. "They had self-propelling talent."

Monsey acted fast. In June 1996, six weeks before the release of *Wannabe*, he managed to get hold of a copy of the single's video – and played it 70 times a week on The Box, thus massively increasing its chances of hitting number one in the charts. It was only at the girls' insistence, incidentally, that *Wannabe* was their first release: Virgin and even the normally sagacious Fuller had wanted another track called *Love Thing*. The girls stuck to their guns – and won.

Wannabe was released on Monday, July 8, 1996. It went straight to Number One, knocking Gary Barlow's first solo single *Forever Love* down to Number Three. "I was really pleased at knocking Gary Barlow off the Number One slot because I thought it was a reflection of our times," said Victoria. "Actually, I used to fancy Gary Barlow, after he changed his image... but he doesn't look as if he likes to have a laugh, does he?"

Wannabe stayed at number one for seven weeks, and ended up in that position in a total of 32 different countries. Their follow-up single *Say You'll Be There* also went to Number One, as did the two subsequent releases, *2 Become 1* and the double A side *Mama* and *Who Do You Think You Are*. This meant the Spice Girls were the first act ever in UK pop history to have four

number ones with their first four singles.
Wannabe went into the US charts at number 11,
the highest ever for a European act, and ended
at number one, a first for a European debut.
Their first album, *Spice*, sold over eight million
copies worldwide. The Spice Girls had made it.

Shh**5**hh!

Spice Mania

NINE – EIGHT – SEVEN – SIX – FIVE – FOUR – THREE – TWO – ONE! The crowd, several thousand strong, went wild. It was November 7, 1996, and the Spice Girls had just turned on the Oxford Street lights. Four short months earlier, no one outside the music industry had heard of them. Now they were household names.

As she stood on the balcony looking at the seething mass of fans beneath her, Victoria could hardly believe it. Here, at last, was what she had craved all her life: fame, adulation and success. The Spice riches had not really started accumulating yet but such had been the success of the group in such a short time that there was no doubt they were on their way. "I think the moment it really hit us was the day we had to turn the Christmas lights on in Oxford Street," she recalls. "We went through these barriers and there were policemen and security guards everywhere. We just drove straight through. We looked at each other and started squealing."

It was quite a step up from those days in Maidenhead. All those months of practising had finally paid off, all that hard slog had been put to good use, and the girls were now stars. It was what Victoria had craved from the days when she was still a toddler and had just started learning to dance, through to her adolescent years, when she battled on, determined to attend dance lessons despite the bullying she had to put up with at school. This was the girl who had been practising her autograph since she was a child, and that practise, just like the hours she spent perfecting her dance routines, was finally being put to good use. She was being asked for her autograph now, all right, not least on the night the girls turned on the Oxford Street lights.

There was drama, that night, as well, and funnily enough it also involved autographs. Fortunately, Victoria's mother was on hand to leap into action. Four fans were so overcome with excitement that they had to be taken to hospital and one, an asthmatic, was comforted by Jackie Adams after the police had lifted her over the security barriers and placed her on the pavement to be treated by paramedics. What seemed to be the cause of deepest distress was not her medical condition; rather, that she would not be able to get the girls' autographs. "My mum took her name and address and said we would send her a signed photograph," says Victoria.

During those long days in Maidenhead the girls were wannabes, dreaming of a life in the spotlight, but with no assurance of their future success. Now they were the most talked about band in the country, and, just as the girls had predicted, they were being hailed as the new Take That.

Virgin Records, hardly able to contain itself with joy, said, "Girl power is seeing off the boy bands. The attraction for the boys is obvious because they are five very pretty girls with a lot to say. But a lot of young girls bought the last single [*Wannabe*] as well, because at last they have role models who aren't middle aged and singing about love – they are just out to have a good time." A spokesperson for the HMV chain of record shops confirmed that the girls were, indeed, taking off. "It's incredible. We haven't seen a pop act sell this fast since Take That."

The girls had totally grasped the public's imagination, not least through two highly polished videos that accompanied their first songs. The first, for *Wannabe*, very unusually was shot in one long take: it shows the girls running into a club full of fuddy-duddies and bursting into song as they go. Geri and Mel B kicked off as they told each other what they really, really wanted, Mel C performed back-flips, Emma looked cute and Victoria smouldered as they ran amok amongst the much older residents of the establishment. They were good but there was still the odd moment that proved they were new to all this: Geri, for example, can be glimpsed checking her position is where it should be before taking the next dance step.

Victoria didn't actually feature too heavily in this video – her starring moment comes when she is discovered sitting on the knee of a bishop – before the girls whisk her away to dance with them again. The look is already in place, though: the short skirt, the heavy make-up and a greater air of sophistication than that possessed by the other girls – although to be perfectly honest, at that stage of their careers, that wasn't saying much. Her relatively small role, though, may be the reason she had a much bigger role in the second video, which accompanied *Say You'll Be There*.

This was filmed in the desert and featured the girls dressed as leather-clad fantasy figures. Resplendent in a black leather catsuit, Victoria looked like a cross between a Bond girl and Catwoman and her character was given a name to match: Midnight Miss Suki. (This was the video that gave David Beckham his first glimpse of his future wife – not only did she catch his eye, but he announced he was going to marry her to the man with whom he was watching the video, team-mate Gary Neville.)

This one actually had a plot: it appeared to involve the girls saving various individuals and possibly the world; men appeared tied up and the girls untied them, before hurling some mystical object into the sky, which went on to shatter vials of water. It didn't bear too close an analysis, but it looked good, featuring Victoria as heavily as the others and it propelled the single, like the first, to Number One.

And in those early days, before the Spice battles began, before there were Spice-divorces (Mel B), Spice-depression (Mel C), Spice-eating disorders (Geri and Easy V herself) and goodness knows what else, it truly felt for the girls as if all their wishes had been granted, with an extra sprinkling of success scattered on top. There was one amazing moment after another, such as the time the girls first appeared on *Top of the Pops*. "It was a dream come true, really," says Victoria, "just because I'd always watched it. I felt like a proper pop star. We were all like, 'Oh my God this is *Top of the Pops*!' We all said we were proper famous people now."

And they were. The Spice Girls couldn't sneeze without it making the front pages. Everyone, but everyone, wanted a piece of the new sensation. This was not always what the girls wanted. Several ex-Spice boyfriends kissed and told, including Mark Wood, who distinguished himself with a lurid account of sex with Posh on a speeding train. "Rock and roll as it sounded and much as I'd have loved for it to be true, it was actually very untrue," snaps Victoria. Inevitably, four of them were caught fibbing about their ages (only Mel B told the truth): Victoria had knocked a year off to become 21. It might sound young to start fibbing about your age when you are barely out of your teens, but remember, these girls were appealing to very young children. Nude shots of Geri and Mel B began to circulate: the two took it on the chin but Victoria, naturally, had nothing to worry about. Sometimes there are advantages to being a goody-goody and this was one of them.

The girls ran riot wherever they went, boasting about the number of men they had sex with (actually, Victoria didn't join in whenever this topic came up, but she looked on approvingly) and generally attempting to out-boor the Gallagher brothers of Oasis. An image was born which, looking back, now seems almost totally unfounded. The girls would whistle at builders, shout "Gerremoff!" at blokes who took their fancy and even terrorise other male bands. It seems remarkable that anyone took this seriously but during that summer's Radio One Roadshow in Birmingham, the girls managed to terrify their slightly their male counterparts in Let Loose and East 17 by mooning at them and threatening to trash their dressing rooms: security guards were promptly installed. It was ladette-ism before ladettes were born.

Then there was the inevitable (and short-lived) flirtation with lesbian chic. Mel B made all the girls snog her (or at least claimed to have done so) when she got her tongue pierced. Geri spoke movingly about her desire for a relationship with a woman and complemented a fellow singer on her "lovely breasts." Victoria did not contribute much to this debate but it's unlikely anyone really thought the Spice Girls harboured Sapphic tendencies, not least because of the glut of kiss and tells from men.

And the girls were even cool. *The Face*, no less, ran a piece about them, identifying Victoria as "a Miss Sophisticated who still lives with her self-made parents in a big converted schoolhouse in the country. She wears a lot of make-up and short skirts and 'all the men want to screw her,' according to Geri. She likes Gucci. She has three Yorkshire terriers and doesn't usually drink." The Guardian also noticed the girls, calling them "Top Shop salesgirls on a diamond nite out" – an appellation that will not have pleased Victoria, given that her penchant for designer clothing was already becoming well known. She was beginning to have the funds to buy her wardrobe herself now, as well, rather than depending on her parents.

Everyone loved the Spice Girls and no one had ever seen anything really like them before.

The Herberts had got the mix absolutely right. Little girls adored them and so did their fathers. Although they were a manufactured band, there was a kind of freshness about them: what you saw was what you got. Sporty Spice really did spend a lot of time in the gym, Baby Spice really was close to her mother, Scary Spice was certainly loud, Posh Spice clearly adored clothes, no matter what the detractors said about her accent and Ginger Spice was, well, Ginger. Ginger Spice was also unofficially known as Sexy Spice, given that Geri had rather more curves then than she does now, which might have led to some friction, especially given the fact that it is now Victoria who is commonly considered to be the most desirable of the girls. But if any of them resented Geri's unofficial moniker, they were too professional to let it show back then.

Money began to flow in. At Geri's suggestion, the girls all bought rings from Tiffany's, with "Spice" engraved on one side and "One of Five" on the other. (Posterity does not record what happened to the rings when Geri absconded, although the other girls were reportedly very upset when they first saw her ringless.) Victoria's family were as thrilled as Victoria herself, following her progress up the charts, around the world and into the nation's hearts and minds.

"My mum always has the latest magazines ready for me when I arrive home," said a breathless Victoria, as she got used to her new celebrity. "She keeps all our press cuttings and sometimes buys two copies of each magazine in case we're on both sides of the page." Victoria's mother did get upset, though, when she saw unflattering remarks about her pop star daughter, although in the early days, these were few and far between. Everyone was so taken with this new set of public figures that any mention of eating disorders, cosmetic surgery and pop-star tiffs was still a long way ahead.

The girls were everywhere, literally. One minute they were touring Japan, the next attending the Smash Hits awards in December where, five months into their time in the spotlight, they won three awards. *2 Become 1*, their third single, easily made it to the all important Christmas number one. December also saw an interview in the normally highbrow *Spectator*, a magazine more usually interested in politics than pop personalities, and, for neither the first nor the last time, the Spice Girls delivered the goods. The magazine wanted them to talk about politics – and so they did, regardless of the fact that they were backstage at the Brit Awards at the time. It turned out that they had a hitherto unnoticed political bent. Victoria, it emerged, is a Eurosceptic. "The whole European federal plan is ridiculous," she announced. "We are patriotic. The single currency is an outrage. We want the Queen's head – or the King's head if we've got one – on our coins."

Victoria, whom the author of the piece, Simon Sebag Montefiore, identified as the Bill Cash of the Spice Girls (Bill is a highly Eurosceptic Conservative MP), then continued, "It's been a terrible trick on the British people. The Eurobureaucrats are destroying every bit of national identity and individuality. Let me give you an example, those new passports are revolting, an insult to our kingdom, our independence. We must keep our national individuality."

The interview becomes increasingly entertaining as it goes on, as well as giving an early clue to Victoria's outspokenness. At the time, given her image, she was considered to be cool, quiet and aloof. For the *Spectator* interview, in which she did a good deal of the talking, she was anything but. Margaret Thatcher ("the first Spice Girl") and Sir Winston Churchill are both cited as influences on the Spice ideology and Spice music. Is this, asks Sebag, a reference to Sir John Colville's memories of Churchill singing Harrow School songs in his bath during the war? "Yeah, partly," says Victoria, who was even showing signs of having a good sense of humour.

She also had strong views about the dismantling of the House of Lords – she was against it. "Earls and dukes are good for tourism," she said. "We admire marquesses as British ornaments." The girls were then questioned about the possibility of a hung parliament (this was six months before the election that catapulted New Labour into power.) "If we were a party, there is no way we would form a government with Labour," Victoria stated categorically. "No. Providing we had consulted with our members, we should indeed contemplate sharing power in a coalition with John Major."

Not that Victoria was overly smitten with Major. "He's a boring pillock," she muses. "But compared to the rest, he's far better. We'd never vote Labour… But the good thing about Major is that because he has not got any personality, he's not hiding behind some smooth façade. He can't rely on his looks, can he?" As it happens, John Major went on to say almost exactly the same about Robin Cook, implying that he, too, had read the article. And the real villain of the piece turns out to be Sir Edward Heath. "If Ted Heath was the man in power who tricked the English into voting for a federal Europe when they did not mean to, then that is bad," Victoria declares. The interview made headlines across the national press – and the first Spice Girl, Baroness T, sent her admirers a Christmas card.

In all these sentiments, incidentally, Victoria is fully supported by at least one other Spice Girl. Geri famously switched allegiances by appearing in a Labour Party Political Broadcast in the run up to the 2001 election: Victoria expressed no preferences that time around but given the cars, properties, jewellery and all-round wealth she and Beckham had acquired by that time, one suspects "Toria" is still a Tory at heart.

This was not to be the girls' only brush with politics. Shortly after the interview was published, it emerged that Labour Party Leader Tony Blair was in the girls' bad books because he had turned down an invitation to appear in the video for *Wannabe*, possibly because he was aware that one of his predecessors, Neil Kinnock, had received a great deal of criticism for appearing in Tracey Ullman's video *They Don't Know About Us*.

That did not mean, though, that the soon-to-be Prime Minister held the girls in low regard, or that his advisors were not fully aware of the importance of being in touch with youth culture. In the run-up to the 1997 election, he was able to name three Spice girls – Victoria, Mel C and Geri – while the incumbent PM, John Major, could name only two. They were Mel and Geri, but given he didn't specify which Mel, it was generally felt that Blair had well and truly won this crucial battle for the heart and soul of the British electorate.

No item was too small to escape notice back then. The fact that the house in which the girls lived in Maidenhead had gone on the market for £92,500 made the news: "It needs decorating but that's no reflection on the girls," said estate agent Paul Tandy. All the locals suddenly remembered them. "I had to tell the little blonde one off for chucking rubbish in the road," said neighbour Pam Parks.

Spice, the album, was released in October 1996: in true rock and roll style it turned into a battle of the giants, with the Spice Girls up against Oasis, no less. The girls won. Spice opinions were sought on every matter. Victoria confessed that her "fave food" was finger buffets, and her "top totty" was Ray Liotta in the film *Goodfellas* – of course she hadn't met David yet.

Their management lost no time in making everyone aware of the new Spice status. Muff Fitzgerald was doing PR for them at Virgin Records and put the following message on his answering machine: "If you're calling about the Spice Girls, they will be unavailable for interview for the next six months and we will not be able to satisfy your demands. Their diaries are also full, so if you are inviting them to a charity do, film premiere, any function or the opening of an envelope, they will not be able to attend." The message was clear: give us some respect.

As it happens, respect really was due, given that the girls were now being hailed as the saviours of the British music industry. There was an 11.5 per cent increase in record sales between July and September 1996, according to the British Phonographic Industry, with overall sales up to £225 million. And who had burst on to the scene in exactly that time? The Spice

Girls. Prince William, of all people, was spotted buying their debut album although he was said to prefer Baby to Posh.

And no one could quite believe how, well, wonderful the girls all were. All right, so everyone recognised that *Wannabe* and its successors, while catchy, saleable and highly polished were not exactly high art, but it was the girls' differing personalities that were beginning to catch everyone's attention. Geri and Mel B appeared to be the leaders of the gang, but that didn't mean people weren't fascinated by the dark and mysterious looking one in the short skirt. All the girls were beginning to be outspoken: primarily on the subject of Girl Power, but, as the *Spectator* interview revealed, they could chat about pretty much anything when called upon so to do.

By February 1997, the girls were mixing with the celebrity equivalent of royalty. They made a video for Comic Relief featuring the song *Who Do You Think You Are*, in which a group of look-alikes, headed by French and Saunders, try to shoulder the girls out of the way in order to perform themselves. Jennifer Saunders was shadowing Geri, while Dawn French was Victoria's double: "Is it like looking in a mirror?" cried the famously voluptuous Dawn, encasing stick thin Victoria, who was dressed in a silver catsuit, in a most un-Gucci like bear hug. "Well is it?"

The girls continued to go from strength to strength. They were invited to launch Channel 5 in March, which they did with a rousing rendition of *5-4-3-2-1* reworked as *1-2-3-4-5*. "Like us," said a cheery Channel 5 spokesman, "they are tongue in cheek, young, fun and very modern." Not everyone in the country could actually get the new channel at the time, of course, and neither was it then clear that the channel's output would be considered in some quarters to be a little dubious, but so what? The launch made the headlines, the girls and Channel 5 both garnered valuable publicity and a good time was had by all.

Soon it was time for the conquest of North America: they were making waves in the notoriously hard to crack United States market with a seeming ease that could only leave their rivals (such as Oasis) looking on in impotent fury. In February, *Spin* magazine said, "Unless a new sensation arrives in the next few minutes, Spice Girls are the new Nirvana." The new Nirvana, no less. Could life get any better than this?

Yes, as it happens, it could. In the same month, *Village Voice* commented, "Their excess spunk already has allowed them to transcend their manufactured roots... the Spice Girls are Madonna x 5 and their debut sets the stage for their future as confidently as the Material Girl's glorious first LP..." This reference to Madonna was very apt. All the girls adore her, have a good deal in common with her and met her on their American tour – apart from Geri, who had left by then – but Victoria, more than the rest was a Madonna wannabe. She didn't flout her sexuality in anything like the way Ms Ciccione did, but like Madonna, she possessed a formidable amount of determination. She knows it, too. "I'm proof that if you want something enough, you can get it," she says.

That was not all. *Entertainment Weekly* chimed in: "What lifts the Spice Girls above female Bay City Rollers status is that *Spice* [the album] is a devilishly good pop collection, as the girls deploy their thin, snarky voices in the service of white hip-hop that's not without soul..." Not bad for a first time act in the US. The Spice Girls really were making the grade and now they were discovering that their appeal extended to the United States as well. To succeed in the way that they had in the UK was difficult enough, but to make it in America was thrilling. And, even better, America was thrilled in return.

It was also in the course of the early part of 1997 that Victoria had another, not entirely successful, stab at rock-star behaviour. Filming a sequence for a German television show, the group were introduced to a band called 3T, comprised of three boys called Taryll, TJ and Taj. Among other claims to fame, the trio are nephews of Michael Jackson. As they were performing, Victoria ran out on stage and pulled down Taj's trousers.

It turned out that nephews of Michael Jackson, who are also stars in their own right, do not like their dignity to be assaulted in this way. Taj and his brothers were absolutely furious. They demanded the performance be reshot, after which they marched out of the studio in an extremely bad temper. Victoria being Victoria wanted to apologise, to no avail – the boys, like the boy bands in Birmingham the previous summer, had taken refuge behind their security guards and were refusing to acknowledge the boisterous girl band. Again, looking back it seems incredible that five noisy girls could so unnerve a trio of highly experienced performers, but there were the halcyon days for the Spice Girls. If they wanted to terrorise boys then they would terrorise boys, and everyone else had to play along with them.

Behind all the fuss, though, it was less a rock and roll lifestyle than a military one. The girls had an extremely tight schedule which they stuck to at all times, and when you're under that kind of pressure there is no chance at all of a John Lennon-style 18-month-long lost weekend. The only release Victoria could manage was the odd afternoon shopping at Gucci. Not that she would have wanted to leap into a lifestyle full of sex and drugs and rock and roll, anyway. She went into the music business to become famous, not to get off her head every night and that was yet another reason some parents of her young friends were only too pleased to encourage adulation of the clean living Miss V.

"Victoria's too vain to do drugs," declares one close associate. "Lots of people do drugs because they have too much money and not enough to occupy their time. Victoria has lots of money but far too much to occupy her time. It wouldn't even cross her mind to take drugs or even to drink in excess."

Despite this, however, there were some people in the adult community who were not too happy about the influence Victoria and the band were exerting on the nation's six year olds. Little girls were beginning to demand to dress like the Spice Girls and given the fact that the girls tended to dress provocatively, this raised eyebrows in some quarters. There were mutterings about the sexualisation of young children, with some commentators wistfully musing on the days when under 10s played with teddy bears, not CD Walkmans.

And then there were the lyrics of the songs: the little ones might have had no idea what they were singing when they launched into "If you wannabe my lover" but their parents understood and not everyone liked it. (This trend for blaming the Spice Girls for the collapse of modern civilisation hit its zenith a couple of years later, incidentally, when both Victoria and Mel B were single and pregnant: both were promptly blamed for encouraging teenage pregnancies. As Victoria rather irritably remarked, neither were teenagers and both married the fathers of their children, although in Mel's case the marriage turned out rather less satisfactorily than in Victoria's.) The girls were bewildered by the attacks. It was they who were espousing Girl Power, they said. They were encouraging little girls to stand up for themselves, to value female friendship, and to be a success in later life. These fears did not last. Now that the six year olds who so loved them then are about 11 and forgot about the Spice Girls years ago, no one seems to mind.

Victoria was, however, taking to other aspects of fame like a duck to water. Early on, she developed the famous pout, explaining, "I'm not really a big, big grinner anyway, but when we started doing all this press I saw pictures of myself and I hated my smile, so I just found a facial expression that suited me better." She smiles a bit more these days, especially when David's around, but she still likes to maintain that aura of coolness.

And it was perhaps inevitable that her relationship with Stuart Bilton would come to an end. He had been hovering in the background as Victoria's star rose higher and higher but eventually her new lifestyle just became too much and she decided to put an end to the romance. Shortly after Stuart emerged from hospital following a skiing accident, Posh gave him the push in March, 1997. "Victoria told him that being in the Spice Girls meant she doesn't have time for a relationship at the moment," said a friend. The two have remained on good terms and still occasionally speak to this day – and to his credit, Stuart has never been openly critical of his famous ex.

The break-up of the relationship was a shock not only for Stuart, but for friends who had thought they would become engaged before long. As with Mark Wood before him, Victoria might not have told Stuart absolutely the whole story. The split was announced on March 28. But eleven days earlier, on March 17, Victoria had made a new friend. His name was David Beckham.

*Shh*6*hh!*

The Colour of Money – Part I

The Spice Girls had become a phenomenon. Apart from breaking one musical record after another, they were practically unique in their appeal: boys loved them because they were sexy and girls loved them because they could relate to them. In fact, little girls fans actually screamed when they appeared, an honour usually reserved for boy bands, not girl bands. Their polished pop appealed to a good many more adults than cared to admit it, they had been written about in every journal in the land, and they had managed to persuade veritable cohort of British celebrities to appear in *Spiceworld: The Movie*. There was just one nagging question at the back of everyone's mind. How long would it last?

Not long at all, as it turned out. The original line-up didn't even stick together for a full two years after the release of *Wannabe* – Geri walked out in May 1998, an act that the four remaining girls have clearly not been able to forgive to this day. And it now seems that Mel C may no longer be part of the line-up, although reports that she has left are constantly denied. But back then, the worry was not about the group's break-up: rather, it was about how long the Spice Girls would remain at the top of the world. Celebrity is a very fickle companion, and never more so than in the world of pop stardom. And so the question was: how to make as much money as possible before the girls faded back into obscurity?

Simon Fuller devised a strategy, the likes of which had never been seen in the music

Spot the superstars! An early school picture of Victoria (*top*) and David (*bottom*). David is first on the left in the front row. You can see David's father in a blue top, clapping in the back row. *Inset*: Victoria's birth certificate.

Fame never seemed far away for the young Victoria Adams. She attended the Jason Theatre School as a child, where she lapped up the attention on stage; and she was an irrepressible dancer.

Top: Even as a young child, Victoria used to practise her signature in preparation for the time she would become famous!

Bottom: The house where the girls first lived.

Early publicity shots of Victoria taken by Geoff Marchant. These were taken in 1992, four years before the Spice Girls became a worldwide phenomenon.

Like any pretty young girl, Victoria had plenty of boyfriends. Two of them, Nick Stern and Mark Wood are pictured here. But they couldn't have reckoned on the arrival of a young footballer by the name of David Beckham. Here they are pictured at their first ever meeting.

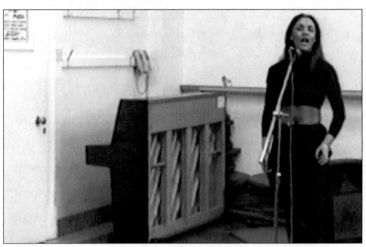

Putting together the Spice Girls was no mean feat. The brains behind it all was Bob Herbert (*top left*). He was tragically killed when his sports car spun out of control. Michelle Stephenson (*top right*) was one of the lucky few to end up in the band, but she was soon replaced by Emma Bunton. But Victoria would become the most famous Spice Girl of all – she is pictured here during her audition for the band…

...and here with the rest of the girls, in an early band shot from 1996.

Victoria's early dreams of fame were soon realised, with appearances as varied as star-studded performances (*top*), and meetings with the most influential people in the world. They are shown (*below*) with Prince Charles and Nelson Mandela.

industry before. The girls would endorse absolutely everything they could, from Pepsi (considered cool in the pop world – Michael Jackson and Madonna had both done it) to Asda (not considered cool anywhere, by anyone.) In doing so, not only did the girls temporarily saturate the market with their presence, they actually managed to make advertisement history, too, in a series of endorsement strategies that were entirely unique to them.

Perhaps the biggest, the most enterprising and the most sophisticated agreement was the £1 million deal the girls struck with Pepsi. It consisted of three layers, the first of which was a 30 second television commercial. Initially the commercial was shot for the UK alone, but eventually became so successful it was shown worldwide. The second part of the deal was an promotion of the product, with pictures of the girls on the cans. Pepsi drinkers could then send in 20 ring-pulls for a Spice Girls CD, which featured four previously unreleased tracks. Pepsi cost 35p a can at the time, which meant that CD, hardly longer than a single, was going for

£7, but as Pepsi pointed out, you did get 20 cans of the drink thrown in on top. At the height of Spice mania, the company was receiving 12,000 CD redemptions a day, and sold an estimated 500,000 in total.

The final part of the deal, and this shows you how complex it was, involved the girls' first ever live performance, to be held in Istanbul on October 12, 1997. Quite apart from the Pepsi angle, this concert was very important to the girls, for industry insiders were increasingly griping that they couldn't *really* dance, couldn't *really* sing and a live performance was the only way to prove their detractors wrong. "We'll show the world we can cut it as a live act," said a defiant Geri. "To all the men coming along to our show, we're gonna tour the pants off ya." At the same time, though, everyone was keen to make sure they had, shall we say, a sympathetic audience, preferably not too close to home should anything go wrong.

And so the location was Istanbul and the audience was made up of completely smitten Spice fans. We can say that with a good deal of certainty, for the only way to get tickets to this concert was to send off to Pepsi for a Spice CD: your name would thus be entered into a ballot and 20,000 lucky fans would get to see their idols on stage. This was also a very good way of keeping out the harsher critics.

In the event, the strategy worked brilliantly: the concert was a great success, the Spice Girls proved themselves worthy of the stage – although they went on to become a lot more polished – and everyone went home happy. Especially Pepsi, who made a lot of money, and the Spice Girls who not only did likewise, but massively increased their profile in South East Asia, a notoriously difficult area for British bands to crack. It did bring it home to Victoria, though, that live performances are very different from working away in a studio. "It was a shock," she admits. "By the third song I was absolutely knackered."

Unusually, the campaign was aimed specifically at pre-teen children, which was another very good reason for using the Spice Girls. "We did a big deal with Pepsi and the people there were mostly against it," remembers Simon. "They said, 'It's too young, we wanna be hip and happening; 17 to 24 year olds, that's where we want to be.' And for me as an entrepreneur I couldn't understand that. Seventeen year olds have no money to spend; all they're interested in is getting pissed and shagging. What do they care about Pepsi? You want six year olds to identify with Pepsi. Global branding works like that. Why do adults drink Ribena? Because they drank it as kids and they love it. That's clear cut. It's amazing how many companies haven't figured that out."

Larry LeBlanc, Canadian correspondent for *Billboard* magazine, points out that in many ways, this strategy harked back to Frankie Avalon and Connie Stevens, both stars in the 1960s and both with successful careers based on television appearances. The Spice Girls, along with groups such as Backstreet Boys and Aqua, hark back to that era simply because they appear on television as much through their advertising work as through anything they have actually sung. "Don't forget their appeal has largely been garnered by television – all these acts," says Larry. "They're all video-friendly acts and they're good looking kids, all of them."

But this time round, of course, the target audience was younger. "The thing that has happened in the last two or three years is that record company people have woken up and said, 'Wait a minute, we have not been servicing the eight to 12 year old marketplace,'" says Larry. "What you're talking about really is an awakening of essentially an audience that was disenfranchised 10 years ago as all the companies ran off and tried to sign grunge bands."

The next deal, for which they also earned £1 million, was for Walkers Crisps. Walkers was also not considered too naff, not least because Gary Lineker had done a long running and highly successful series of ads for the company. In July 1997, Walkers launched a new Cheese & Chives range of crisps and a limited number of packets featured our heroines. It also ran a promotion giving consumers the chance to win £100,000 and a range of Spice Girls memorabilia including jackets, CDs and lapel badges. On top of that, the girls appeared in two television ads with Lineker himself. Again, the strategy was a great success: Cheese and Chive sales boosted Walkers' share of the crisp market up six per cent to 45.5 per cent, while Walkers Crisps sales shot up by 14.5 per cent. Girl Power was officially cheesy – but it was working.

And so it went on. The girls got £750,000 for advertising Polaroid: a special edition Spice Camera came out on the market, and the girls did advertisements for the camera and rolls of film on MTV. It is rumoured that the deal included a clause giving the girls £1 per Spice Camera sold. Then they got a further £1 million for a SpiceWorld Playstation game, released in the run up to Christmas, featuring five songs and video clips.

So far, so good, but it was at this stage that eyebrows began to be raised about the products the girls were endorsing – not because there was anything wrong with the products themselves, but was this really rock and roll? For an estimated further £1 million, the girls advertised

Asda: they endorsed more than 40 products in the run-up to Christmas 1997 from cakes to a "Spicey" pizza. There was no television this time, but their pictures appeared on packaging and bill boards.

Then there was a campaign for a body spray called Impulse Spice, for which they earned an estimated £500,000. It later emerged that enticing shots of the girls' figures, which appeared in television and cinema commercials, were actually body doubles. Next there was Chupa Chups in which the girls got an estimated £250,000 for promoting a wide range of products, including a ball containing 48 lollipops with a bubble gum centre and candy coat. And this was not all. The girls endorsed a lot more: Cadbury's chocolate, Unilever fragrance and any number of official products from duvets to dolls. The girls also applied to the Patent Office to have their names and associated catchphrases registered as official trademarks, although to be fair, that was also to stop other companies from taking advantage of them.

By this time it began occurring to everyone, not least the girls themselves, that this was all going far too far. It's one thing becoming a household name, but when your name begins appearing on every product in the household, the novelty value soon wears off. Speculation began that this was a case of overkill seeing off the original product – the Spice Girls themselves. And, as with everything concerning the girls, this immediately became news in itself. It wasn't exactly a case of questions being asked in the House, but everyone took an interest: *Marketing Week* ran a cover story called "Over Spiced."

"Has any music property ever been as cynically and wholly exploited as the Spice Girls?" it asked. "It is not just the T-shirts and magazines or even the blanket tabloid coverage. What is unprecedented is the number of brands lining up to jump into bed with the fab five." It promptly listed the brands and then went on, "This is all for a group which has never performed live [the piece came out just before the Istanbul concert] and has produced only one album – albeit one that has brought four number one UK hits. But the rash of deals has less to do with the hysteria that engulfs seven year olds and more to do with the realisation that this could be the last Christmas for the fab five." That prediction turned out to be rather wide of the mark, but by this time the *Financial Times* was weighing into the great debate. "As the Spice Girls' commercial image proliferates," it thundered, "some fear their fortune might be short lived."

When even the *Financial Times* started fretting about the girls' future, something had to be done. The solution was obvious and in the traditions of Girl Power, the Spice Girls took matters into their own hands. They sacked Simon Fuller. Matters had come to a head in November: not only did he have them promoting far too many products, but he seemed to have turned into the caricature of himself as played by Richard E. Grant in *Spiceworld: The Movie*. The girls complained that he was working them to the point of collapse.

"They are exhausted and they don't see why they have to keep piling on the work," said a source close to the band at the time. "They don't think they are going to fade away and feel there is plenty of time to make more money." Rick Sky, an expert on the music industry added, "I think there are two possible reasons why the Spice Girls have decided to sack Simon. The first is that they are working too hard and want to take life a bit easier. In my experience money is behind these kind of break-ups."

The second reason might have been this: namely that Simon was having a relationship with Emma Bunton and that this was upsetting the status quo within the group. Geri became particularly irate about this, demanding that Emma should choose between the girls and her man. There were also reports that Mel B had been seen screaming furiously at Bunton. Both Emma and Simon subsequently denied the story, but whatever the truth of it, Emma stayed with the band and Simon didn't. On that occasion at least, friendship didn't end.

And there were other tensions. Simon had floated the idea of the girls living abroad as tax exiles, which would have meant spending at least six months a year out of the country. Victoria, who had a new boyfriend, a footballer called David Beckham, was particularly opposed to that idea.

The girls, especially Geri, credit one man with giving them the strength to sack Simon and that man, believe it or not, was Nelson Mandela. The girls were doing a tour, drumming up publicity and support from all over the world, and had, in the course of five weeks visited Granada, Delhi, Singapore, Tokyo, London, Cologne, Paris and, of course, Istanbul. They ended up in South Africa where there was a meeting with Mandela and Prince Charles – who, not for the last time, was covered in Spice kisses and had his bum pinched – and it was that meeting with Mandela that gave the girls the strength to act.

At the time, though, it had all seemed very jolly and informal. Asked how it felt to be so close to five beautiful women, Nelson Mandela replied, "I do not want to get too emotional about it. These are my heroes. This is one of the greatest days of my life." Prince Charles, getting into the spirit of the thing, announced that this was the second-best day of his life. And what was the first-best day? asked a reporter. "Meeting them the first time," he said (at a Prince's Trust concert in Manchester six months earlier.)

The ending for Simon, when it came, was both carefully planned and brutal. On August 26, 1997, each Spice Girl had set up her own production company. Victoria's was called "Moody Productions". Then on September 1, each girl demanded to be made a member of Spice Girls Limited, the company set up to take on the world (and handle the Spice Girls careers.) This gave the girls financial control and placed them in a position whereby they could sack their management company if they wanted. They did want to and they soon acted – just a couple of months later, when Simon was in Rome recuperating from surgery on his back. For a time until, ironically enough, she left six months later, Geri became _de facto_ manager of the band.

It's hard to recall now quite what a shock this sent through the music industry. The Monday after the sacking, shares in EMI, which owns Virgin Records, fell as a direct result of fears about the girls' future. Funnily enough, Virgin itself was not unhappy, given that Virgin executives had signed the girls up to sell records, not crisps. "The general feeling is that the Spice Girls have been marketed successfully to the detriment of the music. And that's down to Simon," said a Virgin outsider. "Where is the music in all this work for Walkers Crisps and whatever else?"

And there were clear signs that the pressure the girls had been under was beginning to show. "It's all gone very weird. They've been sleeping together," said Julian Henry, Fuller's assistant. "No. Not sexually. Just like sisters do. And when outsiders visit, they go into a huddle, like a rugby team."

At the time, there were reports that Simon was shattered and thought the girls had stabbed him in the back but time has clearly healed many wounds. "Without sounding totally crap, it was just one of those things," says Fuller. "It wasn't that dramatic. Someone called me, I was in Italy and said, they don't want you to manage them any more. I was like, OK, fine. If that's what you want, let's sort out the deal, and it was all done in 24 hours. I've seen Geri since and it was totally cool, because what can you say? It was their prerogative."

The deal in question was his payoff. Industry insiders put it at £20 million, which must have gone some way towards softening the blow. And Simon's career hasn't exactly suffered: among many other things, he went on to manage S Club 7 and Hear'Say – who rehearsed in a house, many have since pointed out, that was a good deal more luxurious than the Spice residence in Maidenhead. Simon says that his only regret on splitting with the group was not to have masterminded a "megatour." "I always thought the world tour was gonna be the end thing," he says.

This period was a low mark in the band's history. About a week after Simon left, they were booed off stage at the Onda awards in Barcelona. The problem was that there were photographers present and the girls – who by this time were getting control-freakish about their image and had a clause in their contracts saying they would not be photographed while they were singing – weren't pleased. A stand off ensued.

Eventually, late and with grim expressions, the girls marched on to the stage to perform *Spice Up Your Life*, but the mood had turned ugly: boos and catcalls eventually forced them off the stage. "When they didn't appear on stage, I just wanted to die," says Eva Cebrian. "We believe in the freedom of the press and you can't just push photographers out. They know they are not so pretty and they want to control their photos." It was not a good week.

Of course, after Simon's departure, rumours were rife that the band was about to split up. The girls were having none of it. "We will always be Spice Girls when we are 60," protested, of all people, Geri. "We want to be together forever." But for the moment, at least, they were getting on with it. The Spice Girls' second album *SpiceWorld* had been released just before the sacking and although US sales were not quite up to expectations, it stayed at number one in the UK for three weeks. The film was about to be released, their television show "An Audience With The Spice Girls" had done well, they cleaned up at the *Smash Hits* Poll Winners' party and they even took part in the Royal Variety Performance. Their friendship wasn't to last forever, but for now, at least, it was business as usual.

And the next item on the agenda was *SpiceWorld: The Movie*. The film, which had been shot in six weeks on location in London and Los Angeles, received an extremely lacklustre reception from critics and there is no doubt it was not *Citizen Kane*. It wasn't even *A Hard Day's Night*, The Beatles' first film, to which it bore a slight resemblance. "One of the worst movies ever made," said one of the harsher reviews. But despite the reviews, to view it now reveals a film that was a good deal funnier and more enjoyable than anyone was letting on back then. Nor could it be classed as a failure in any way. Serious critics subsequently were rather kinder, it cost $10 million to make and grossed $75 million and it got a very glitzy premiere in Leicester Square with Prince Charles gamely allowing himself to be mauled again by the girls, who were as overexcited as ever.

Ironically, *SpiceWorld: The Movie*, had been written by one Kim Fuller, Simon's brother. This was not, however, nepotism at its worst: Kim had been in the business himself as a writer for a good 20 years, cutting his teeth on *Not The Nine O'Clock News* and going on to write scripts for the likes of Lenny Henry, Rory Bremner and Tracey Ullman. And it shows, because the film's script is genuinely amusing – silly, yes, but amusing. The plot, if it can be dignified thus, involves five days leading up to a Spice concert in the Royal Albert Hall, the tension being created by the problems that pop up along the way. Will they make it to the concert hall on time? The answer's not that hard to guess but there is a certain ingenuity to their various plights.

For a start, there's a documentary team headed by Alan Cumming following them around. (The documentary team don't actually hinder them, but they're still there.) Then Barry Humphries plays an evil tabloid editor called Kevin McMaxwell (a very famous tabloid newspaper editor was called Kelvin McKenzie and an equally infamous tabloid proprietor was called Robert Maxwell), who enlists the aid of an evil papparazzo to split the girls up. Meanwhile, the girls' manager, played by Richard E. Grant, is driving them increasingly hard, allowing them no time off, as well as being pitched at by a couple of Americans producers, who want to make a film involving the Spice Girls. (Given what happened with Simon Fuller, the brother of the man who wrote the screenplay, it is more than a little ironic.) As the real film wears on, its plot begins to resemble the plot within the film being pitched, which is not just clever but positively post-modern – for the Spice Girls.

There are encounters with aliens in a scene which first looks like a parody of *Close*

Encounters of the Third Kind but turns out to be an illustration of the fact that the girls' fame has now reached outer space. Roger Moore is in there as well, playing a record mogul-cum-James Bond style baddie (first he strokes a white cat, then a white pig) and somewhere in the middle of all this, the girls have to look after a close friend. She is with child but deserted by her boyfriend, so the girls look after her for, as we all know, friendship never ends.

And finally, like the Partridge Family, the girls travel around in a huge bus, except theirs is immense and covered in a huge Union Jack. It also has Tardis-like properties, in that it's much bigger inside than it looks from the outside and all the girls have customised sections: Baby, for example, sits on a swing while Posh has her own catwalk. And the mix, although ludicrous, is highly enjoyable. (Richard E. Grant might not wish to know this, but it's his second best performance after *Withnail and I*.) And as an example of the girls' then pulling power, it's impressive: along with the cast list already mentioned, we get glimpses of Sir Elton John,

Bob Geldof, Meatloaf, Jennifer Saunders, Michael Barrymore, Martin Stuart, Stephen Fry, George Wendt, Jools Holland, Hugh Laurie and others too numerous to mention. There were 22 stars (excluding the girls) in total.

There were funny echoes of the girls' real life as well. An article in the US newspaper *The Sunday Sun* commented, "Their manager, played by Richard E. Grant, is a monstrous and ruthless manipulator, and Stephen Fry gives them a lecture on the backlash which successful artists must expect. It so mirrors their recent crises that cynics might suggest events were manipulated in order to boost the movie. 'It would be a good publicity stunt,' agrees Mel C, although Mel B spoils it by adding, 'We're not actually that clever' and Geri brings us down to earth, explaining, 'The whole thing is a parody. Everyone thinks Victoria never smiles and is a measly old Posh Spice, but she has a wicked sense of humour.' Victoria brightens briefly. 'We take the piss out of ourselves and the media. At the end of the day we take our music very seriously, but we're not afraid to laugh at ourselves.'"

It was also around this time that Posh was outed as not being as Posh as she'd like to be. These revelations came from, of all places, *Tatler*, the posh person's bible. They took Victoria to Paris, dressed her up in haute couture, put her on the cover and quoted her verbatim. The pop princess turned out to be slightly less regal when discussing royalty: "When we met Charles, we was all really, like, cheeky with him. At the end of the day, prince or no prince, he really does sit on the toilet like everybody else. You've just got to picture him with nothing on."

Not content with installing that alarming image in the readers' minds, Posh vigorously defends her Posh credentials: "Listen, I don't speak that badly! It's only 'cos I'm tired, for a start." before anxiously discussing the merits of her nickname. "She says that sometimes, at home, she was called Tor by her family," read the interview. "'But that's very posh,' I say, thinking of all the Sloaney Tors I meet, and she asks excitedly, 'Is it? My boyfriend calls me Tor as well, is that Posh?'" Finally, she goes on to upset her new boyfriend's boss, Alex Ferguson, to say nothing of millions of Manchester United fans. "Not many nice shops in Manchester," she observes. "No Prada and Gucci in Manchester." Moments later she realises what she's said – "Oww! Naoww!" and vainly implores the magazine not to print her remarks: very meanly, it does. It also comments on her very heavy make-up, possibly a hangover from the acne she suffered from in her teens.

By this time, towards the end of 1997, the girls were estimated to have earned a staggering £8 million each. They had risen above jibes from fellow artistes directed at their marketing activities – Phil Spector called them "the Anti-Christ," which seems a little extreme – and were now ready to start their first ever world tour. And here there was no sign at all of waning popularity. When they kicked off on February 24, 1998 in Dublin, at an 8,000-seat arena called The Point, tickets were changing hands for up to £125, five times their face value. Victoria sported a new, short hairdo, and her new fiancé was in the audience.

The girls were a revelation. The Istanbul performance, although deemed a success, was but a pale forerunner of what appeared on stage. They pulled no punches: arriving on stage with state-of-the-art computer graphics playing behind them, which one observer described as a cross between *Cabaret* and *Oklahoma*, the girls went through three costume changes in the first act alone. Another two followed in the second, the dancing was as polished as the singing, with five Spice boys shadowing the girls and the show lasted a total of two hours. They were on the road.

The girls were also witty in their stage costumes: in India, they donned saris for their performance. By April, the girls had hit Glasgow, their first ever British date, where they performed in front of a 9,000-strong audience. By this time there were seven Spice Boys, one of whom very nearly performed a full monty on stage. "When you're on stage, it's the most amazing feeling," says Victoria. "When you've got the fans singing the songs you've written, going, 'Yeah, go for it!' that's what keeps us going... as well as each other."

It seemed as if nothing could go wrong. Something did. The first hint that anything was amiss happened in May, when the Spice Girls were scheduled to appear on the BBC's midweek lottery programme, before flying out to Scandinavia. The girls appeared – minus one. "Geri's not very well tonight," Mel C explained to viewers. "She had a stomach upset which turned into a virus, and the doctor said she shouldn't do the show." Victoria, who was becoming something of a peacemaker within the group, actually tried to get hold of Geri, but with no success.

The girls then flew out to Oslo, again minus Geri. Alan Edwards, spokesman for the band, was very reassuring. "After that [the concert] the girls have a 10 day break before they gear up for their American tour, so hopefully she will be fit for that. Geri has got very run down over the last week or two. She got a stomach upset and it has knocked her for six." But rumours were beginning to circulate that something was really wrong. Before the Lottery show, the girls had been performing in Helsinki, and were seen having a heated row as they left their hotel.

Geri had also featured in two news stories that week: one about a breast cancer scare and the other about a meeting with television presenter Chris Evans (photographers had been tipped as to the timing of her arrival.) The rest of the girls were said to be angry about both stories, not least because they said they hadn't been told about them in advance. They were also angry about reports that Geri was now considering a career in television.

It soon became known that Geri had in fact left. She'd fled to Paris with her brother. It seems that tensions within the group had reached breaking point, and her constant rows with Mel B – really a fight as to who would become the leader of the band – had finally gone too far. In her autobiography she explains that despite all her fame and wealth she felt unfulfilled, as well as adding that she knew the girls could go it alone, but at the time it was an absolute crisis.

The American leg of the tour was due to start on June 15, with 40 dates set up and fans expecting to see five Spice Girls, not four. There was intensive speculation that the band would have to split up, that Geri would be sued by the US promoters and that the tour would not go ahead. Reports said that at the end of the tour, the band would split up and the girls would pursue solo careers – with the exception of Victoria, that is, who would be content to settle for married life with David Beckham and any children who might come along.

The girls, however were made of stronger stuff. For a start, it suddenly occurred to them that all this speculation as to their future was engendering valuable publicity just at a time when their rival girl band, All Saints, had seemed to be on the verge of overtaking them. Secondly, they could do it. These girls had now been rehearsing together for four years and were easily able to share out Geri's lines between them, while adjusting their dance routine. They lost no time in putting out a statement.

"We are upset and saddened by Geri's departure," it read, "but we are very supportive in whatever she wants to do. The Spice Girls are here to stay – see you at the stadiums! We are

sorry to all our fans for having to go through all of this. All our love, Victoria, Emma, Mel C, Mel B. Friendship never ends!"

Shh**7**hh!

An Angel in Adidas

As match reports go, there was nothing out of the ordinary about this one. "Manchester United, appropriately enough in front of Spice Girls Mel C and Victoria, showed the rest of the Premiereship that they [the other teams] are in danger of remaining frustrated Wannabes," wrote Matt Dickinson in the *Sunday Express.* "Not even form side Wednesday could come close to upsetting the champions after a brief, early flurry. The only blemish for the Premiership leaders was a thigh strain for Andy Cole, which is almost certain to rule him out of Wednesday's European Cup trip to Oporto."

And so it went on. The headline read, "Cole goal adds Spice to Premiership race," but other than the first paragraph, that was the only mention of the famous girls in the crowd. There was no mention at all of David Beckham. The date was March 17 1997 and Victoria was still going out with Stuart Bilton – a relationship that was to end within a week. When Victoria sees what she wants, she goes out and gets it.

And although Victoria has never been interested in football as a game, it would seem that she has always had a penchant for footballers, as her childhood friend Emma Comolli recalls. It was while Victoria was still attending junior school that her parents became even more wealthy as a succession of businesses flourished. "Victoria's parents were both very hard working, says Emma. "Once they decided to do something they worked like Trojans until it was a success. I remember they used to go to charity events for successful business people in which they often met famous footballers.

"Victoria did not know anything about football. She was a good netball player, but she really liked footballers even then. Her Mum and Dad would be on orders if they went to one of the dinner and dances involving Tottenham Hotspur to come back with autographs of the players. She had ones from people like Ossie Ardiles and Steve Perrymen. She had no idea what position they played but she liked keeping the photos in her pink bedroom because they were famous."

As it happened, it would be some months before Victoria's new boyfriend was named in the press, but the aforementioned match report was the first indication of what was to come. For the time being, the world-famous pop star and the world-famous footballer were behaving like gauche adolescents, as recalled by David Beckham in *My World*. "When the Spice Girls first appeared, all the lads had their favourite," he wrote. "One of my mates used to say, 'Geri's the one. Geri's definitely the one. Look at her, yeah,' and I'd say, 'No believe me, the one with the dark hair, the bob, is the one. The one with the legs.' Then Victoria turned up at a football game in London. I sort of said hi, but she was more forward than I was and came up to me and said hello. Then the Spice Girls' manager at the time introduced us properly. I'm a shy person, so I still only managed to say hello and then turned away. I was cursing myself afterwards because I just couldn't believe that I'd wasted my big chance."

As it happens, Victoria had also had the hots for her husband-to-be, well before the pair actually met. "I remember doing an interview with a soccer magazine and they showed me photos of different footballers," she says. "Then I saw his picture. I just remember thinking one word – gorgeous." (As it happens, Beckham was not the first footballer to catch her eye. Victoria was rather embarrassed when it later emerged that she had once had a crush on Beckham's team-mate, Ryan Giggs. Rather confusingly, Ryan went on to date Lisa Rys-Halska, who was an old girlfriend of Becks'.)

And indeed, the star-crossed lovers were not to remain apart for long. A couple of weeks later, David spotted Victoria again, this time at a match at Old Trafford – the match at which the Spice Girls were spotted. For a woman with a total lack of interest in football, she'd developed a sudden enthusiasm for the sport and it helped that Manchester United was Simon Fuller's team.

After the match, she and David bumped into each other in the players' lounge. David went all bashful again, but Victoria clearly felt that it was time she took matters into her own hands: she marched up, engaged him in conversation and then asked for his phone number. This David refused to divulge – because he was afraid she wouldn't call him – and demanded hers instead. "When I got home I wrote her number down on six or seven pieces of paper so I wouldn't lose it," he says.

Victoria's sister Louise also remembers the meeting. "I was with Victoria when she first met him," she says. "We were at Old Trafford and were both really drunk. Myself and David's sister Joanne were talking and trying to get them together. It was a case of, 'Oh, my sister really fancies your brother' and vice versa. We found out after that he'd seen her on the *Say You'll Be There* video and said he wanted to marry her."

Armed with her number, David leapt into action. He rang her first thing the next morning, learned that she was going away the next day, wanted to ask if he could drive down to London to see her, lost his nerve, rang back, asked if he could drive down to London to see her and drove down to London to see her. The next problem was that they couldn't go out together as the paparazzi would see them and tell everyone they were a couple. So they ended up going round to Mel C's house, where the timid David was petrified for two reasons: firstly Mel was a Spice Girl and secondly she was a well-known Liverpool fan. Victoria, not very surprisingly, did all the talking. "Can you imagine what he's like to go on a first date with?" she asks. "Even more shy."

It was not long at all before love blossomed as the couple continued to meet in secret. They eventually managed to have a real date: they went to the cinema to see *Jerry Maguire* and

David agonised over whether it would be acceptable to hold hands. "At the cinema," he confided, "I tried to put my hand on her knee but I didn't want to be too forward on our first date, so I pretended I'd done it by accident. We were," he continued, with possibly the understatement of his career, "like two nervous teenagers." It was not until the fourth date that they finally kissed. "I'm glad I waited," says David. "It was a great kiss."

Actually, the attraction had been massive and mutual from that very first meeting. "I could see he was shy," says Victoria. "I found that really attractive." David, meanwhile, was a bit nervous that the pout signified displeasure. The Victoria forgot herself and started beaming. "As soon as she smiled I knew it was going to be OK," said Becks.

One anecdote illustrates the early stages of their courtship. It was a sunny day in London and Victoria and David were out pursuing their favourite hobby: shopping. But they weren't shopping together – they had gone out separately to pick outfits for their date that evening. This was the summer of 1997, less than a year after the Spice Girls hit Number One with their first single *Wannabe*, and only a couple months into Victoria and David's relationship.

Suddenly, David's mobile phone rang. It was Victoria. "Let's meet up quickly now, before you come and pick me up tonight," she said. David agreed. He drove to the lay-by where Victoria was parked and pulled up beside her. Victoria jumped out. She was carrying a huge bunny she'd bought for David in Harrods, which she gleefully gave to her new man. Dumbstruck but delighted, David took the bunny and headed back to the car. Victoria watched him go. "Nice arse!" she cried.

To the outside observer, David Beckham is a man full of contradictions: to paraphrase Sir Winston Churchill on the subject of Russia, he is a riddle, wrapped in a mystery inside an enigma. To see him on the football field is to see a highly intelligent player on the loose: to chat to him afterwards is to chat to someone who does not, in many ways, seem to be all there. It is startling to hear his voice for the first time: it is quite childlike and hardly wavers in tone at all. On the other hand, however, Beckham took on the responsibilities of a man early on and has stuck to them: there is nothing childish about his marriage to Victoria and he is clearly a wonderful father to Brooklyn.

It is Victoria who gets angry about the thick and thin jokes: she says that Beckham is an intelligent man and she may well be right – it's the voice that lets him down. In *The David Beckham Story*, broadcast in 2000 on ITV, Beckham is seen fretting about his forthcoming appearance on *Parkinson*. He is worried, he says, not so much about Parkinson tripping him up as in not being able to understand Parky's long words. "I'll listen to the little ones around them," he murmurs anxiously. Truly, he does himself no favours. In that reply he comes across as being a few strikers short of a football team – but if you could imagine someone with a highly expressive voice saying it – Stephen Fry, for example – his words would appear to be self-deprecating and witty.

The other strange facet to his character is that he is clearly extremely vain. He says he wants to be seen as a footballer rather than a model, and yet he sometimes seems to spend half his life gazing into the camera with a pout to match that of his wife. Before she met him, Victoria always said she wanted a man who looked good and knew how to dress. In Beckham she got that in spades. When they first met, Beckham was brunette and floppy haired, he swiftly moved on to blond and floppy haired. (After watching him in a match on television, Victoria once famously told him to get his roots done.) Since he has sported a shaved head, saying the inspiration for the look came from his captain and mentor Roy Keane.

His next manifestation, the infamous, high-fashion mini-mohican, was copied by children all over the country and in the midst of all this, there has been a succession of goatees, to say nothing of sarongs and other sartorial style statements. ("You'll look like a big Jessie," said his father when David told him he'd been snapped wearing something that looked like a skirt).

Nor does David behave like a typical footballer. He is, by all accounts, a good cook, he is perfectly happy being a gay icon, he may or may not, depending on who you believe, wear his wife's underwear, he helps look after Brooklyn and he has spoken out against homophobia and racism. Given the boorish attitudes amongst British football fans, all of this makes David either extremely brave or extremely stupid.

The secret to it all, strangely enough, is that he and Victoria have an extremely passionate love life and it is the confidence in his own very robust sexuality that gives him the courage to stand up for gays and racial minorities. (Victoria likes to hint at this: before she had Brooklyn she said happily, "I'm practising to get pregnant!") The passion between him and Victoria is still there: they can't be in the same space without touching each other, curling up around each other, holding hands and nuzzling and marriage and parenthood have done nothing at all to put a stop to that.

In retrospect, it isn't surprising at all that the two fell in love. They have an enormous amount in common. For a start, both were extremely close to their families: when they were introduced at Old Trafford, David's family was also there. Then they both achieved fame and riches at a very young age, had to cope with the spotlight early and, of course, are two utterly driven characters. Victoria, as she is the first to admit, may not be the greatest singer of the age, but she got to the top by sheer hard work and determination. David, on the other hand, probably is the greatest footballer of his age, but becoming the England captain does not happen without a certain amount of determination on anyone's part.

David Robert Joseph Beckham was born on May 2, 1975 to Ted, aka David Edward Alan Beckham, an East End gas fitter and Sandra Georgina Beckham née West, a hairdresser. The couple had been married in 1969 and David has an older sister, Lynn, and a younger sister, Joanne. The family initially lived in Leytonstone, East London, before moving to Chingford in Essex, where David grew up.

David's talent was obvious from a very early age. Ted was a huge football fan and encouraged his young son to take an interest in the game from childhood. He also planted in David a passion for Manchester United. David was not, shall we say, an academic boy, but he worked extremely hard at developing his footballing skills. Every night after school he would go to his local park, Chase Lane, to practise. He joined a Sunday League football team, with the highlight of the week being training on Wednesday evening.

In 1986, at the age of 11, David's talent proved to be as strong as his ambition. He won a soccer skills competition at Old Trafford, organised by Manchester United footballing legend Bobby Charlton. The prize was a trip to Barcelona, which, ironically enough, would become the scene of his greatest triumph, the victory in the European Cup against Bayern Munich in 1999.

As a young teenager, Beckham played for a local side, Ridgeway Rovers, before going on to train with a number of London clubs, most notably Tottenham Hotspur, where he stood out because he always turned up in a Manchester United shirt. This pleased David's grandfather, who was an avid Tottenham fan and had insisted on buying him Spurs kits every Christmas – but the young David wasn't interested. So, when at the age of 16, he finally had to choose between Tottenham, Arsenal or a move to Old Trafford, there was truly no choice. David was Manchester-bound.

Following David's arrival at Manchester United, he made his way swiftly up through the youth and reserve teams. Becks hit the spotlight in August 1996, when he scored a wondergoal against Wimbledon at Selhurst Park. "When I score from way out, people often say it is a freak goal, but it isn't," David protests. "I have worked at taking shots at goal from way out since I was a kid… It is only by practising that you get to score the spectacular goals which give you such a buzz. The long-range shot at Wimbledon is my all-time favourite. I remember seeing Neil Sullivan off his line and thinking I might as well go for it. I didn't even think to look where I was on the pitch. It was only when I saw the video that I realised how far out I was. That video tape has got a bit of a hammering. I've still got the boots somewhere. I never wore them again after that goal."

Victoria might not have known anything about football, but she did know about long hours of practise and determination. And Beckham was even seen as an oddity in childhood, just as Victoria was. Victoria was bullied for, among other things, slaving away at ballet school; David got teased about his intense attachment to football. On Michael Parkinson's television show, he admitted he used to get a bit of stick because, while his mates spent Saturday night drinking and hanging around street corners, he would be tucked up at home watching *Match of the Day*. When we were fifteen we started going down the pub," says Richie Sutton, who knew Beckham as a boy. "David didn't come because he wanted to go to the park and play football."

And it wasn't long before the couple's similarities in character were being manifested in a physical way. "We've got matching dogs, matching watches and similar wardrobes and I like that," said Victoria, after they had been together for a while. "I mean, I know it's really tacky, but it makes us laugh."

She recognised these similarities right from the start. "Everyone used to ask if my initial attraction to David was the fact that he was famous," she says. "I always said it wasn't but that was actually a lie. If someone is really talented, as a footballer or an artist or an academic, the point isn't that they are famous, but they are talented and dedicated. The fact that we are in the same position makes us equal and it is quite ironic the way our careers run parallel. When we first met I was on my first album and he was playing in his first proper team season... We are equally famous and attract equal attention."

And happily enough, they both enjoyed the same kind of lifestyle. "Like me, he'd rather cuddle up on the sofa with a takeaway than be out at a club," she says. "Most of the time we spend together we stay indoors and I wander around with no make-up and just a tracksuit on."

As for David, after meeting Victoria, he gave every impression of having been swept off his feet. "This is the first time I have been in love," he declared. "And once you meet that person, you want to spend the rest of your life with them. You dedicate your life to them. You never hurt or destroy that relationship."

Another similarity between the two is that they are capable of taking the abuse that goes with the job and getting on with life. Victoria doesn't care about seeming tacky and is the first to own up to limited talent: Beckham, on the other hand, is perfectly happy for people to call him thick and mock his silly voice. "I only open up to those I'm close to," he says. "I have inner parts that people can't get into. I'm a person who likes to keep himself to himself, believe it or not. I also know that people say, 'That Beckham's thick, ain't he?' and they take the mickey out of my voice. But they don't really know who I am."

Back in the beginning, however, Victoria didn't know really know who he was, either. But she was perfectly happy to find out. Knowing that it would hit the headlines as soon as they were outed as a couple, the pair managed to keep their burgeoning relationship under wraps for the best part of two months. "We managed to keep it quiet for the first eight weeks," says Victoria. "We used to go out in disguises – hats, glasses, all sorts of ridiculous clothes – and it worked."

Gradually and inevitably, however, news of the relationship began to leak out. The couple were seen together in a nightclub over the Easter weekend, and then Victoria took him home to meet the parents on that Bank Holiday. And even if they hadn't been spotted, Victoria's demeanour hinted that something was afoot: she had that unmistakeable air about her of a woman in love. "She is walking six feet off the ground at the moment," said a friend at the time. "She says David is the most handsome man she's ever met." Finally, in May, the couple appeared arm in arm in the drive of David's Cheshire home: they helpfully cavorted in full view of the cameras before retiring back inside. It was official: Posh and Becks were in love.

By June, the pair were talking openly about the romance. They were speaking on the phone every day and making no bones about it: "That's normal. She is my girlfriend," said David coyly. "I'm a footballer and she is a Spice Girl. It would be silly if we did not think the media and public were attracted to us. But we are just two normal young people going out together. It helps that Victoria is famous. It helps with the pressure if she is involved because we both share it."

And the pressure of attention was something the two had to learn how to cope with – and fast. "We do understand the pressure, even though we are only 22 and 23," said Becks. "We are learning together. I don't see myself as front page news but going out with Victoria, I am going to get it. It is something we must handle."

It didn't hurt that the two shared a mutual interest in their appearances. David made a splash when he turned up at a London fashion show in Gucci loafers and no socks: Victoria was delighted. "This is what I've always said, 'if you wanna be my lover, wear a pair of Gucci loafers.

I do like a man who dresses well. But that's the problem – men are my biggest weakness."

Actually, that accolade probably goes to clothes. David and Victoria's time together invariably involved shopping, with Prada and Gucci being Victoria's favourites. "My shopping binges remind me all the hard work is worth it – because I often get depressed," she rather unconvincingly remarked.

The relationship quickly intensified. Both were travelling a good deal, but kept in constant contact by telephone. "I dread to think about the phone bills he has run up on this trip," said a Manchester United chum when Beckham went to Germany to play in the European Cup and Victoria was on a promotional trip to the United States. Victoria, meanwhile, consoled herself by sleeping in Beckham's England football shirts. "She gets so lonely on these tours she sleeps in the shirt and it makes her feel closer to him," her mum Jackie told a friend.

One person who was not so delighted about the relationship and the effect love in the spotlight was having upon young David, though, was Sir Alex Ferguson, the gravelly voiced manager of Manchester United. Sir Alex had been cultivating David for the best part of a decade and was dismayed to see his protégé haring up and down the country and spending time off concentrating on telephoning Victoria rather than honing his football skills. "What I think is hard to control a little bit," says Sir Alex, "is that the publicity machine from her side – from Victoria's side – has been interfering with his life and you know, you can't have that. You've got to be in control of your situation, you're a footballer, it's different... There's nothing worse than picking up a paper and thinking, 'Oh Christ, where is he now.'"

David had had a number of previous girlfriends – among them Lisa Rys-Halska, an air stewardess, and two models, Leoni Marzell, and the Italian Stephanie Lyra – but nothing had ever been like this. Nor had Victoria's men meant the same to her. ""I've had boyfriends before," she said. "I've even thought I was in love before, but I was wrong. I've never felt like I do now. I've never been this complete. I'm only 23 but I feel like I know what's important in life now – and it's not getting a discount at Gucci! I know some people think I've got no depth. That of all the Spice Girls – I'm the miserable cow with the pout. But that's all part of the Posh Spice thing – it's not me. I don't mind people thinking that way and I understand that's my image. But there is a lot more going on in my head."

So happy was she, in fact, by this time that the next set of rumours to do the rounds had Victoria thinking of leaving the Spice Girls. This was unlikely. The girls may or may not be still together, they may or may not perform as a group again, but Victoria Beckham had been working for this time in the spotlight throughout her entire life and nothing, not David Beckham, not the future Brooklyn Beckham, not Sir Alex Ferguson, nothing was going to make her give up now. "At the end of the day I don't want to be seen as a footballer's girlfriend," she once said. "I know a lot of them are really, really nice girls, but I want to be known as me."

Not that she was underestimating her good fortune in finding fame, riches and David Beckham. "I'm very lucky," she says. "I've got someone who treats me really well, is really considerate and down-to-earth as well. I'm the first to admit I've said I never wanted to go out with a famous person [*sic*] but that's what David is. He isn't going out with me because I'm 'Posh Spice.' Half the time I see him, I look anything other than posh! We're on the phone a lot and when we do see each other it's quality time. If a relationship is meant to work it can work no matter how difficult it is. Anyway, I can just pick up the papers or turn on satellite TV to see him!"

Crucially, David had the full approval of the Adams family, without which no boyfriend could ever hope to make the grade. "David would be welcomed into our family," said Victoria's mother Jackie. "He is such a decent guy. I couldn't ask more of my daughter." By August, it briefly looked as if David had already joined the family when the couple were spotted wearing matching gold bands on their wedding finger. The pair claimed, however, that these were merely love tokens before Victoria had to jet off on yet another promotional tour. "I miss Victoria when we're not together," said David plaintively. "We get very little time together – and that's hard." To make up for it, the two were showering each other with jewellery and it was by no means a one way process: David was the happy recipient of a Cartier watch and £1,000 Gucci suit.

And he was becoming resigned about the amount of attention they were attracting. "I know dating Victoria has doubled the media interest in me," he said. "We like to go for quiet meals together but we always seem to be photographed shopping. I sometimes think people must think I live in Gucci and Prada shops. I worry that fans will forget I play football as well as go out with a Spice Girl. But I've turned down a lot of sponsorship offers because I want to be known as a footballer, not a model." (One offer he did not turn down was from Brylcream – shortly beforehand, he had signed a £1 million sponsorship deal.)

There was, however, a big downside to all this. Given that Becks was becoming as famous a boyfriend as he was a footballer, fans were beginning to taunt him about the relationship as time went on. Jealousy was plainly the cause. Becks was a good looking, rich man who drove an £80,000 Porsche and had a good looking, rich girlfriend. They would chant obscenities about Victoria when he ran on to the field, which prompted words of support from Sir Alex Ferguson, who is not otherwise known as Victoria's greatest fan. "Top players will always get that kind of stick, but they grow up at Manchester United understanding it's the price they may have to pay for playing here," he said.

"The entire team get stick, but some players take more than others and now David is under the spotlight. I've not spoken to David about it and I don't plan to either because it's not affecting him, because he's such a good player. Now that Cantona has gone it seems to be the likes of David and Roy Keane who are the targets. But I have no worries about whether they can handle it – I know they can."

David took it fairly well, although on occasion he could be seen shouting back. Victoria's reaction couldn't have been cooler and less concerned. "Fifty thousand fans singing, 'Posh takes it up the arse,'" she recalls without a hint of self pity. "My dad said, 'What's that they're singing? And the lady next to me offered me a sweet."

The wedding rumours were intensifying. Victoria was spotted at a bridal shop in Goff's Oak and rather snappily denied that the two were engaged. Some time later it emerged that what really annoyed her was the implication she'd buy a dress from a local shop rather than Gucci. (In the event, a couple of years later, it turned out to be Vera Wang.) David was constantly being asked if and when the two would be tying the knot: rather than issuing any denials, he would giggle.

Christmas rolled around. David and Victoria jetted back to Manchester from Dublin, where they had been staying at the exclusive Kildare Hotel, to take up residence in two adjoining suites a local hotel, the Rolls and the Royce.

One was used as a sitting room and the other as a dining room: Victoria's parents came up from Hertfordshire to join them. Among other presents, the two gave each other Rottweiler puppies named Snoop Doggy Dogg and Puff Daddy. "They want something to cuddle when the other one isn't there," explained a friend, adding that the dogs lived mainly at David's house. Victoria also got a £13,000 cross.

And so it surprised no one when a short ten months after that first meeting, David popped the question. The couple decided to get engaged while Victoria was on tour in America, and, fittingly, it was all done in the best traditions of romance. They were reunited at the five-star Rookery Hall Hotel near Nantwich, Cheshire, on January 24, 1998: Victoria had flown in from Los Angeles, where she'd been promoting *SpiceWorld: The Movie*; David had just been playing in Manchester United's 5-1 FA Cup fourth round victory over Walsall. "We came here straight after the game and ordered champagne and dinner in our room," Victoria said the next day. "We were sitting there in our dressing gowns when David pulled out the ring, got down on one knee and said, 'Will you marry me Victoria?' I said yes, then produced my own ring and said, 'Don't forget girl power – will you marry me?' I'd chosen the ring with my mum and dad in Los Angeles." Overjoyed, the newly engaged couple rang their parents – and then got in touch with their PR people.

A hasty photo shoot was arranged for the next day. David and Victoria nearly overslept, and so appeared a little disconcerted when they showed off the rings. David had presented Victoria with a £40,000 solitaire diamond, designed by Boodle & Dunthorne. Victoria had reciprocated with a £50,000 six carat, diamond encrusted gold band from a jewellers in Hollywood. "It's lovely. It's my dream ring," said Victoria showing off the rock. "It's just what I wanted and it was a big surprise." And how did she feel about the engagement? "I'm all embarrassed now," said Victoria, looking a little coy. Her husband-to-be added that he was "very happy."

They were slightly less happy a couple of days later, though, when Victoria received a

£3,000 bill from Customs & Excise. She had waltzed through the Nothing To Declare channel at Manchester Airport and the first Customs knew of the ring was courtesy of that photocall. It was a "misunderstanding" said a spokeswoman for the band. "She temporarily brought the ring to England before sending it back to the States to be refitted.

"Although it's actually unclear if there's any tax due on it now, Victoria's representatives have settled with Customs officers in advance of any difficulty. An agreement was reached in the last few days. If it turns out she doesn't actually owe any money, the £3,000 could be returned. As far as we know, Victoria is aware of the situation, though she hasn't dealt directly with it. It's all been handled by lawyers and accountants. She's far too busy rehearsing in Dublin for the world tour." And so honour – and the ring, which some alarmists had feared might be impounded – were saved and Posh and Becks launched into their eighteen-month engagement.

But before the wedding could take place, of course, a third member of the family came along

in the form of Brooklyn Beckham. Victoria hinted at it as soon as she and Becks got engaged. "My boyfriend is a football player," she confided to a German newspaper. "We are getting married soon. And as soon as Gucci makes clothes for expectant mums, I would even consider a baby."

Shh **8** *hh!*

Bumps,
Babygros
and Brooklyn

It would be a while, though, before that
marriage could take place. The girls were in the
middle of a world tour and nothing, not even
Geri's abrupt departure, was going to change
that. And, having played their way through the
European leg of the tour, it was time to take on
America.

In June, just before they left for the US, the
girls performed with Luciano Pavarotti in their

new line-up as a foursome. The occasion was a concert in aid of the charity War Child in Modena, Italy and despite the events of the last two years, the girls still found their fame a little unreal. "Last month we stood on stage with Pavarotti and an orchestra behind us," said Victoria wonderingly when they had reached the States. "I remember us lot stood in a line like that down the dole office. It's mad."

More madness was to come: Spice fever was running as high in the United States as it was in Britain and the rest of the world. The girls had visited America on numerous occasions before to do promotional work and had even filmed the video for *Say You'll Be There* in the Arizona desert. But this was different. This was an 11-week tour, with over 40 live performances in 35 cities and no Geri – the girls were still in a state of shock at her departure. They were recovering enough, though, to be able to start hinting that while she had done very good work as a spokeswoman for Girl Power, stage performances were a little more, well – "It wasn't her strongest thing," said Victoria sweetly.

The girls had ruled out finding someone new to become fifth member of the band and also had no plans to replace Simon Fuller, who they had dismissed the previous November. In one of those rare moments when the hype actually matches the reality (and unlike the early days, when they were put together by a group of men) this really was a sign of Girl Power in action. The girls were managing themselves, each taking responsibility for a different area. "We know our own market and what our fans like," said Emma in an interview with all the girls that took place in Palm Beach, Florida, where the tour started out. "We'd rather handle it ourselves than give it to some older person who hasn't got our involvement. I think people would be really shocked at the amount we do."

The others started to chime in. "We all do an equal amount," said Victoria, "handling the area we're best at. Like, Melanie B is tour monitor." "I do personnel and charity," said Emma. "I do merchandising and sponsorship," said Victoria. "And I, like, do the record company, what we're going to record and videos," said Mel C.

And so the girls set off across America, Victoria missing David quite desperately and receiving flowers from him every day. There was a video team in pursuit making a documentary that, when completed, was called *Spice Girls in America: A Tour Story*. On watching this documentary, three main factors stand out. First, the girls truly know how to put on a live show, second, the strain of their workload is really beginning to show – Emma is shown complaining that she's fed up and wants to be at home having a barbecue with her mother – and third, David and Victoria really are passionately in love. David joins the girls in New York after they had been apart for two months and the two just can not leave each other alone: Victoria sits on his knee, drapes herself around him, hugs him from behind as they walk along a corridor together and then disappears altogether, followed less than a second later by David. The two return looking pleased with themselves.

The girls noticed differences between American and European audiences. "The audiences over here have been amazing," said Victoria. "It's funny, because when we were performing in Europe we'd see a lot of kids dressed like all of us. But out here, the kids dress like Spice Girls – and so do the mums. You'll see a 45-year old woman dressed like Baby Spice in a little skirt and pigtails. I've seen a few Posh Spices. They do it all right but they always have the dodgy clothes on when they're being me."

The tour was also proving to be exhausting. When they were in Europe, the girls sometimes managed to go home for the odd day in between gigs but in America that simply wasn't possible, provoking sustained bouts of homesickness from all of them. "I miss my family more than I thought I would," said Victoria. "I mean, it's great to go out for glamorous dinners, shopping and things like that but there's a bigger part of me that would rather stay in with my family and have a takeaway. When you can do what you want to do, you realise what you really enjoy doing. Sometimes it's difficult when you're in America and all you want is a cuddle."

On the positive side, the girls were also discovering one of the benefits of getting rid of Simon Fuller. They were able to take the odd day off and rest in between gigs. "We do get a little tired, but we get time off," said Victoria. "The schedule now is our schedule, because we look after ourselves. And it's good fun. That's what keeps you going. But it's hot out here. We're performing at a lot of amphitheatres – half indoor and half outdoors. Coming out in a PVC catsuit in 100° F isn't that comfy."

As the tour progressed, Victoria's fellow Spices began to notice a change in her appearance. She had started vomiting regularly and was looking pale in the mornings. She had also developed a taste for the oddest food – most particularly gherkins. And, very unusually for Victoria, she was putting on weight. Could it be that she was carrying a child?

Victoria had been getting increasingly broody for some months now. Her sister Louise had given birth to a baby daughter, Liberty Lawrence, and Victoria had been overwhelmed at her appearance. "When I saw Liberty, I couldn't believe how tiny and beautiful she was," she said. "It was amazing to hold her in my arms. Usually when I hold babies I feel worried, but not with my own niece. I felt far more comfortable. I even changed her first nappy."

Victoria was in California when the news of her pregnancy broke, and, in the company of her mother Jackie, who had flown out to support her, Victoria spoke of her delight. "The baby wasn't planned, but I never for one moment considered not keeping it," she said. "Why would I? I love David, we are getting married and would have had children fairly soon anyway. I'm over the three months now and I don't mind everybody knowing how happy I am."

It cheered David up, too. Beckham had just had one of the most traumatic experiences in his career, when his petulant behaviour in the June 1998 World Cup, which was taking place in

France, resulted in his being sent off. Following an altercation with the Argentinian midfielder Diego Simeone, which led to David lying face down on the pitch, Beckham flicked up his leg as his opponent walked past. Simeone collapsed into a heap on the ground. The score was 1-1, and England were considered to be on top – until Beckham's sending off. Argentina eventually won 5-4 on penalties.

England fans rose up as one against him, expressing absolute fury at Beckham's behaviour. Even Glenn Hoddle, the England manager, refused to talk to him in the dressing room afterwards. "David Beckham reduced England's chances to cheap metal by an act of crass stupidity," wrote James Lawton in the *Daily Express*. "Please don't hate him," begged Victoria from New York, where she had watched the match, but for now, at least, the golden boy's reputation had been seriously tarnished.

"This is without doubt the worst moment of my career," said David at the time. "I have apologised to the England players and management and I want every England supporter to know how deeply sorry I am. I only hope that I will have the opportunity in the future to be part of a successful England team in the European Championships and the World Cup."

The apology was not enough. A wave of hostility washed over the country to the extent that Beckham's hero, Sir Bobby Charlton, urged the fans to cool off. "You can not throw him to the wolves," he said. "I saw him straight after the match and he was terribly affected by it. He realised what he had done. Someone has to take the blame and David Beckham will take the blame this time."

Even this was not enough: the abuse began to take a sinister turn and at the beginning of the next season, an effigy of Beckham was strung up near Upton Park, home of West Ham United. All things considered, it must have been a great relief for David to fly across the Atlantic into the waiting arms of the pregnant Victoria. "Their reunion in America was the most romantic moment I've ever seen," said a source very close to the group.

"David was close to tears when he held Victoria in his arms. So much had happened since the last time they saw one another, they were totally overwhelmed. He had been through a lot after the shame heaped on him over England's World Cup exit but he was more concerned about her and the baby. He wanted to brush aside the heartache and celebrate the fact that he was going to be a dad. He wanted Victoria to know she and the baby were the most important people in the world."

And David was absolutely delighted about the prospect of being a father. "When I told David I was pregnant, he just started weeping," says Victoria. "He must have cried for about an hour and I had tears running down my face, too. It was a very emotional moment for both of us. The baby wasn't planned so it was a surprise mixed with real delight."

Predictably, onlookers took the news to herald, yet again, the demise of the Spice Girls. Victoria was in Houston when this was put to her: "A lot of people are saying when we go home, that's going to be it," said Victoria wearily. "That's such an English thing to say. Right back to when we first came out – 'Five girls? That'll never work.' But we continued. Then we sacked our manager. 'Oh, that's the end of the Spice Girls.' We got through that. Then Geri left – 'It'll never work.' One of the girls is pregnant – Shut up! I don't want people to read all this negativity."

Victoria also displayed the pragmatic approach that both enabled her to deal with stardom and helped her to protect her fiancé from the jibes that continued to plague him in the wake of the World Cup. "David came out to see me in America after the World Cup," she said. "Obviously it's difficult when people are using your head as a dartboard. He was upset because some bloke made 20,000 red cards for his first big game of the season. I said, 'David, do you know how long it takes to cut out a bit of card? You should be really flattered.' You know what matters – at the end of the day it's my family, friends and David."

As it turned out, Victoria was not the only gestating Spice Girl. Mel B announced she was pregnant too, by one of the dancers accompanying the tour, Jimmy Gulzar, and the two got married in September 13 1998 – a marriage that was to last not much longer than the pregnancy. After returning to England, the girls all took a fortnight off before performing in Sheffield and Wembley after which, as the true pros they are, they completed the world tour. They did, however, postpone the release of their third album, which had been scheduled for a June 1, 1999 release.

David and Victoria's parents were delighted by the news and not concerned about the fact that Victoria was having her baby first and then getting married. Victoria, however, was irritated by some of the press coverage that said the two events should have happened the other way around. "My parents are very, very supportive," says Victoria. "They knew I'm in a stable relationship. At the time myself and Melanie got blamed for a lot of teenage pregnancies but how on earth can people blame me for teenage pregnancies when I'm 25, I'm getting married, I'm in love with somebody and I've got a supportive family? Financially I'm in a good position but that isn't the most important thing. The most important thing is love."

It was around this time that newspaper reports surfaced linking David to a Page 3 girl and a lap dancer, although they stopped short of saying he had had an actual affair. Both David and Victoria furiously denied the stories, calling them "ludicrous" and a set up: they took legal action against the News of the World and won. "I'm glad I've been successful in my own right and not had to use people," said Victoria pointedly (a sentiment with which her erstwhile band Persuasion might not agree.)

"As for David and I, we're very strong and this hasn't damaged us at all. All we're worried about is what tie David is going to wear for the wedding, because we're trying to plan that for the moment. Right from the beginning we've talked about this happening – and I'm surprised it hasn't come up before because, wherever we go, there are always guys who try to talk to me and girls who try to speak to David. But we trust each other."

And the Spice Wagon rolled on. "It was hard when I was on tour, because in the first three months you get a lot of sickness – me and Melanie found it quite difficult," said Victoria at the time. "But I'm getting a proper bump now! It's just so exciting. Mel and I are waddling into the studio, helping to write the third album. It's been a bit strange, because all the girls will be talking about this and that. And then there's me and Melanie saying, 'Oh, I bought this great babygro the other day or, 'How has your scan gone?' Melanie and I ring each other up whenever we've had a hospital appointment and we compare bumps, too, – because we're both getting pregnant in different areas. The other girls have been great, too. We were in the studio the other day doing a B-side and they said, 'Right, you sit down, rest your legs and when you're ready we'll put a chair in their for you to get up and sing!' And they just let me sit there and eat all day."

Other than that, pregnancy did not cramp either of the girls' style. To the clear delight of their fans, Victoria and Mel B both turned up to put in a rousing performance at the 77th Royal Variety Show in December 1998. The Spice Girls sang *Goodbye*, their latest single, before heading off for a night on the town at Marco Pierre White's Titanic restaurant although David wasn't there – he was playing for Manchester United against Bayern Munich. Victoria showed she had lost none of her sartorial flair: she wore a two piece which showed off her bump for the performance and a figure hugging gown afterwards.

There was, however, the odd note of drama. On the way home from a Spice Girls concert in Sheffield, David and Victoria stopped at a service station to satisfy Victoria's craving for sweets. A brawl broke out when someone tried to photograph her: Beckham punched him and the two had to be separated by the police. The photographer then attempted to follow them, leading to a high-speed car chase. But every pregnancy has its own problems.

Brooklyn Joseph Beckham was born on March 4, 1999 at 7.48pm at the Portland Hospital in London, just four hours after Victoria went into labour, and two weeks after Mel B gave birth to her daughter Phoenix Chi in the same place. Weighing in at seven pounds, Brooklyn was born by Caesarean section, because he had turned round into the wrong position just as labour began. "Basically, the baby's head was not in place and it never would have been, so I had a Caesarean, which was all very last minute," says Victoria.

"You have a choice, you can go into labour, but if the head still doesn't engage, you end up having an emergency Caesarean, which can make the baby stressed. All I was interested in was having a healthy baby, and it's funny how suddenly your mind begins to work and all your priorities change. It was like when I was actually in the theatre, I said to David: 'If they take the baby away, for whatever reason, just leave me here, half dead or whatever, and just go with the baby – don't let him out of your sight.' But all the doctors were absolutely fantastic."

The name Brooklyn came from the area of New York in which the couple were staying when he was conceived and Joseph is David's middle name. An ecstatic Beckham came out to greet waiting reporters. "It's brilliant," he crowed. "Victoria is very well. She is sitting up drinking champagne and has spoken to the other girls. It was very exciting but also a little bit scary. There were no complications. It was lovely." And was young Brooklyn going to be a footballer, he was asked? "He has got his dad's thighs," chortled David. "I was there for the birth and it was an amazing experience. We are both overjoyed."

Victoria and Brooklyn stayed _in situ_ for five days, an experience she appreciated. "When I was in hospital, I didn't see all the people that were outside – all the media and the fans," she says. "I was just in there in my own little world, with Brooklyn, and it was lovely. I had the best week of my life."

Victoria's childhood home was the next refuge. Avoiding the waiting fans and press, the family bundled into a limousine with blacked out windows and roared off to stay with Victoria's parents in Goff's Oak. It wasn't long, however, before Victoria was ready to face the public again. Just 10 days after the birth, she, David and Brooklyn went out with her parents, her sister Louise and Louise's daughter Liberty, her brother Christian and Christian's girlfriend. Baby Brooklyn, unlike his cousin Liberty, behaved well.

Brooklyn marked a new stage in Victoria's life. For a start, she took six months off from the Spice Girls and her career, the first time she had done so since the girls got together five years earlier. She was 24 now and a multi-millionairess and even for a woman as driven as Victoria, this seemed the time for a natural break. And she was relishing being a mother.

She provoked more than a few raised eyebrows when she said she could do without a nanny – "I have the kind of job where I can do that. I'll just take it into the studio in a back pack" – and, indeed, a few weeks after the birth she and David were photographed leaving The Ivy, a well known restaurant in central London, looking as if they were walking in their sleep. But the two got stuck into parenthood, David as much as Victoria, and muddled through.

That said, the shock to both, although both were and are besotted with Brooklyn, was enormous. Previously they had been two highly successful people, a pop star and a footballer, with any number of assistants to make sure their lives ran smoothly. When she was on tour, Victoria might have spent some of the time feeling homesick and all of the time missing David, but if she wanted a massage, she got a massage, and there was someone to arrange it all for her. Ditto that with just about anything and in some ways, Victoria had an easy life.

A new baby, however, is a very different matter altogether. For a start, babies require 24-hour attention, a commodity Victoria was more used to receiving than giving herself. And although David was the model father – on the one hand changing nappies, on the other having Brooklyn's name tattooed on his back – looking after a baby came as a real shock to the system. "He was a difficult baby," she admits. "He didn't sleep and he was very, very active all the time. He's like me – I'm always on the phone or doing things. I can't bear just sitting around doing nothing. And Brooklyn's always on the go."

And there were dramas. When Brooklyn was just seven weeks old, he had to return to the Portland Hospital for a hernia operation, although the operation went smoothly and there were no complications. "I was changing his nappy one day and I noticed this little lump," says Victoria. "So we got the midwife round and she advised us to go to London and see his paediatrician. I was really worried, particularly when we found out he had to go into hospital. It was awful when we had to take him down to the operating theatre. But the surgeon was brilliant – you can't even see his scar."

And Victoria suffered from the fears any new mother would have: launching an appeal for the Meningitis Research Foundation in London, she revealed that becoming a mother had made her aware that meningitis is every parent's nightmare – and, in fact, when she got married four months later, one of the options for guests, instead of buying a present, was to make a donation to The Meningitis Trust.

All told, parenthood was fulfilling for both David and Victoria. "We want to be normal parents and enjoy our kids growing up," says David. "There are so many people who want to interfere and destroy it but we are not going to let anyone. We know the people who care about us and, as long as we're happy, nothing else matters."

David was as happy as Victoria to look after his son, as opposed to behaving like one of the lads. "He'll go out for a drink with his friends, which is fine – we totally trust each other so he can do that," says Victoria. "But yeah, I do think he's a bit different. On a Saturday night, maybe, if all his friends are going out, I'll say, 'Well, why don't you go too? If you want to go out with your friends, I honestly don't mind,' and he just says, 'Why would I want to do that when I can sit in with you and the baby and watch a video and get a takeaway?'"

There are also advantages to being a famous parent. "People say, 'Oh you've got all this money, what do you buy?' but the best thing is that money buys you the freedom to be together," says Victoria. "Hand on heart, that's the nicest thing. We're lucky that we can afford to have nice things, and it is quite strange how, when I was pregnant, I got sent a lot of free things. The papers were saying, 'Oh, she can afford to buy a pram and she got it sent free,' but obviously people do get publicity out of us, so that's how it happens. I doubled up on a lot of things so we gave it all to charity."

And just for once, Victoria was relishing the role of homebody. She and Brooklyn were living with David in a plush apartment in Alderley Edge in Cheshire, spending the evenings in and going out to the supermarket like any other young mother. "If anyone wants an autograph, I'll say, 'Not until we've finished,'" she said, "and then I tell the children to say 'please.' David and I want children who are very well behaved." It was not a lifestyle she would wish to maintain for long, but it provided valuable time to get to know her son, as well as recovering from the exhaustion brought on by non stop work since the Spice Girls first got together in 1994.

They did not have a flashy social life. "Both of our families are really down to earth, and we are too," says Victoria. "When people ask what our perfect Saturday night is, we say, 'Sitting in with a takeaway watching *Blind Date*. We're not just saying that; that really is our perfect Saturday night. That and watching *Friends*. You won't see pictures of us coming out of pubs and clubs drunk, having spent the night with loads of famous people. That just isn't us. We met Joan Collins the other day and we were whispering, 'That's Joan Collins.' We're so not cool!"

The £300,000 penthouse flat in Alderley Edge was the couple's first proper home together and it is a shrine to David's career. "David has photographs of his greatest footballing achievements all over the walls," says a source close to the couple. "There are photographs of various goals that he's scored and there's a huge painting of Eric Cantona in a robe – dressed as an emperor. They have lots of scented candles everywhere – it's a very calm, cool, modern sort of flat. Victoria would always pad about the place keeping herself busy. She's like that."

It is a large, open-plan flat, with light wooden floors, centring on a hallway lined with black and white pictures of the Spice Girls on tour. The kitchen has a fake leopard print scatter rug, vertical ladder shaped radiators and a vast Miele oven, used mainly by David. Brooklyn's room is marked by a silver star set in the door.

Victoria also had a good deal to keep her occupied. The wedding, to be held that summer, was drawing near and she was occupied in putting final touches to the arrangements and the dress. And, like any bride, she wanted to look her best for the occasion, which meant being nice and slim. Very slim. Downright skeletal according to some people, in fact.

Victoria has only very recently admitted that she might have suffered from an eating disorder, but there are signs from very early on that she has had an unhealthy preoccupation with her weight. Mark Wood, her first boyfriend, relates how she was always convinced she was fat, even when she was a teenager. And in the early days, Simon Fuller kept a paternal eye on his young charge, on one occasion telling her off in a Hong Kong restaurant for laying down her chopsticks too early and persuading her, gently, to eat some more.

"She doesn't eat properly," says a source very close to the couple, "and that's really frustrated David at times, but it's all linked to the amount of time she puts into her career. She has had ups and downs with her health."

After a baby some women have trouble getting the extra weight off: not Victoria. She only put on a stone during her pregnancy to begin with, but it more than came off. Before Brooklyn's birth she weighed about nine and a half stone, perfect for her height of 5'6. She looked svelte in pictures, with the occasional hint of voluptuousness. She was not skinny, but she was slim. Some months after Brooklyn was born, when revealing pictures of her in a variety of micro minis began to circulate, she almost looks gaunt. She had lost two stone and it showed: where once her legs had been shapely, now they were merely thin. Her shoulder bones showed through her skin and she looked older than her 25 years. Severe weight loss, after all, is very aging. But Victoria refuses to admit that anything could be wrong.

"She's lost loads of weight," says a friend who has spent some considerable amount of time with Victoria. "The problem was that she saw so many pictures of herself so many times that she became over critical of the way she looked. There was a point after her wedding when she was worried she got too skinny and started putting weight back on again. Then she started to look much healthier and full-figured than she had in a long time.

"There's no doubt at all, though, that she's committed to dieting. I'm not sure if she's ever been bulimic or anything like that, she just doesn't seem to eat. She does lead a very busy life, she's very highly strung, she's always dodging around from place to place and there's not always time for food in her schedule. It's not a healthy way to be, but there's no doubt in my mind that she has done some rigorous slimming over the years."

Her appearance would suggest so. Victoria's hip measurements are reportedly just 27 inches, a statistic that is more suitable for the body of a young boy than a grown woman. Victoria reacted angrily to reports that she lost far too much weight after giving birth to Brooklyn. "It's irresponsible to say I'm dieting and anorexic," she snapped. "After a baby you are dashing about all day. I never had a chance to sit down." She claims to eat up to five packets of low fat crisps a day, while her mother said at the time that she saw her eat three bowls of cereal for breakfast. The ever loyal Louise chipped in: "Obviously she has lost a lot of weight since Brooklyn, but she has been eating really healthily and looks great."

The issue has refused to go away and one of the strangest aspects to it is that Victoria lends credence to the stories by wearing extremely revealing clothes that show exactly how skinny she is. Were she to cover up a little more, no one would know that her bones poke through her skin but she doesn't, so we do. This might be because Victoria has a distorted image of her own body, according to one expert in the field.

"Women who flaunt their bodies – even when they're painfully thin – often have a distorted way of looking at themselves," says Dr Raj Persaud, consultant psychiatrist at the Maudsley Hospital. They don't see themselves as thin. That is vital to understanding why they may look unpleasantly thin and then appear to be parading themselves. It is worrying because a distorted body image is often one of the integral features of an eating disorder."

Of course, the pressure on Victoria to look slim is enormous and she is well aware of the unkind press comment following on from the fact that Mel C has gone the other way and gained weight. However, onlookers believe she has gone much too far, not least because she is surrounded by other women who are also far too thin – the so-called "lollipop ladies" with huge heads on stick like figures, such as *Ally McBeal* star Calista Flockhart. And, according to Dr Persaud, many women are proud of their super-thinness.

"They are often perfectionists, women who achieve their goals and are very successful because they are so relentless," he says. "There are lots of women who try to achieve thinness and fail, or yo-yo, so there is a certain competitiveness in being able to achieve what a lot of women can't. Sometimes these woman see it as a massive achievement, and they are very proud, so they wear revealing clothes.

"They devote so much time to the goal that they miss the point of it. Women in the media, women whose jobs are linked to their appearance are living in a very competitive environment. They hang around with other very attractive women. Research shows that women in TV and pop and so on tend to be lower in weight than the average woman. They are mixing with women who are thin as well, so it's very easy to get a distorted view of what weight you should be."

Victoria has finally admitted she hasn't always eaten enough, but will not admit to a serious problem. "I'm not anorexic," she says. "I'm not bulimic and I'm not a skeleton. I'm seven and a half stone, very fit and I've never felt better in my life. With the other girls I have a responsibility as a role model. So many people have come up to me while I've been out shopping recently and told me how they lost loads of weight when they had a baby, too. My mum went down from nine stone to six stone after she had my brother. It's just what happens to some mothers. But I haven't changed what I eat or anything. I honestly feel that my metabolism has changed as I've got older and had Brooklyn. I just seem to burn up food faster."

The speed with which she burns up food is accelerating: in recent publicity shots for her new video to accompany the single _Not Such An Innocent Girl_, Victoria is so skinny as to be almost unrecognisable from her first slim and pretty appearance as a Spice Girl. In that video she changes from wearing white to wearing black to wearing white again, and she got extremely angry when discovering Geri Halliwell was doing the same thing for _her_ new video. But her most notable appearance in white came a few months after the birth of baby Brooklyn. It was time for the wedding.

Shh**9**hh!

2 Become 1

It wasn't just a wedding: it was a coronation to the throne of Planet Celeb. David and Victoria had not only arrived – they had written the guide book. The society wedding of the year, that of Prince Edward and Sophie Rhys Jones a month earlier, just wasn't in the same league, as far as the public's imagination was concerned. The real royal wedding took place on July 4, 1999 at Luttrellstown Castle in the Irish Republic. It was either the ultimate in fairy tales or the ultimate in vulgarity, depending on your point of view. There were pageanters, there were doves, there was a costume change by the main participants half way through, the groom wore almost as much jewellery as the bride, there was a fireworks display. Victoria had wanted a big event to mark the wedding, and she got it.

David and Victoria were allowed to marry in Ireland as they had been issued with a special license by the Archbishop of Dublin and it was a lavish affair by anyone's standards. It was organised by Bentley's Entertainments, which appropriately enough for the Crown Prince and Princess of the celebrity world, is owned by Lord Snowdon's half brother Peregrine Armstrong-Jones and was responsible for Princess Anne's fortieth-birthday party at Gatcombe Park, Peter Phillips's twenty-first at Windsor Castle to saying nothing of Sir Elton John's lavish fortieth-birthday bash.

The wedding, for which *OK! Magazine* bought the picture rights for £1 million, had taken 14 months to plan. "Victoria and David had a huge input right from the beginning," says Peregrine. "Wherever they were in the world, I would get samples, fabrics and plans to them and Victoria would often ring me five times a day with ideas and questions."

There was, it must be said, derision from some quarters about the couple's pretensions. David and Victoria had had a crest especially designed for them, embossed with the initials "VBD" – Victoria, Brooklyn and David. The crest turned up on everything: the invitations, the marriage service and even a purple banner fluttering above the guests on the day itself. Experts were called in to analyse the design: it was found vulgar, wanting in taste and the swan was pointing to the right rather than the left.

David and Victoria were, however, blithely unconcerned about their critics and got on with their plans. "So what if the poxy swan is the wrong way?" snaps Victoria. "Does anybody really give a shit? D'you know what I mean? Having your own crest – it's one of them, innit? [tongue in cheek] We're just thinking, it's the biggest day of our lives – we're just going to go over the top and make it entertaining for everybody."

The very first item on the list was finding a suitable location. "Victoria wanted something really private and unique, somewhere green and leafy, deep in the countryside," says Peregrine. "Architecturally speaking, she didn't want anywhere too stuffy." The only problem was that time constraints meant that Victoria couldn't look for the right venue herself and so Jackie and Tony, ever the doting parents, went off with Peregrine in her place. It took over three months before they hit the right spot, but Luttrellstown Castle, just outside Dublin, proved to be it.

The castle, which has 14 bedrooms and its own golf course, dates from 1794 and is set in the middle of 560 acres. It was built by the second Earl of Carhampton, Henry Luttrell, and more recently members of the Guinness family made it their home. Victoria loved it. "She felt the castle had clean lines and grand proportions without being too imposing," says Peregrine.

"Privacy was really important," adds Victoria. "I wanted somewhere that had a big wall around it, so I wouldn't feel paranoid every time I walked past a window. I really liked the fact that all the rooms at Luttrellstown were sunny and it had a happy atmosphere. We wanted both our families to stay at the venue for a couple of days before the wedding and lots of places we looked at were great from the outside but were really grotty inside. But as soon as I saw this castle, I thought to myself, 'This is the place.'"

The couple had also formed a sentimental attachment to Ireland. "We spent a lot of time in Ireland when Victoria started her tour in Dublin and we felt at home," says David. "The people are lovely – the photographers even asked our permission before they took a picture and if we said, 'No,' they went away."

The next item on the agenda was flowers. The wedding was to have a Robin Hood theme, with three main colours: burgundy, dark green and cardinal purple, and decorations were to be made out of greenery, apples, twigs and yards of fabric. Not one but two florists would be required for the kind of decorations Victoria had in mind: John Plested, who did the floral arrangements for the Queen's ruby wedding (a regal leitmotif was to run throughout the proceedings) and Simon Lycett, who had done the flowers for *Four Weddings and a Funeral*. Simon first met David and Victoria the previous January, when Victoria was seven months pregnant with Brooklyn: "When I left, Victoria gave me a great big hug and told me to ring if there was anything I wanted to discuss," says Simon. "They were both very hands-on throughout the preparations leading up to their wedding day."

And, of course, there was the dress. Victoria's favourite shops are Gucci and Prada but on this occasion she chose to opt for Vera Wang, the U.S.-based daughter of Chinese immigrants, whose clientele includes Sharon Stone, Mariah Carey and Alicia Silverstone. "When I was on tour in New York, I met her for the first time," explains Victoria. "I'd seen her work previously – other celebrities that she'd dressed – and I'd always really respected her. But I thought she was such a nice lady, open to ideas, which I think is important: there are certain ideas I've got, little things I'd like to put on the dress and she was really open to that. I couldn't work with anyone that's got a big ego and won't listen to anyone else's opinion."

Well over a year before the wedding itself, Vera flew into London from New York to meet

Victoria and Jackie, make the first sketches of the dress and take fittings. The corsetier Mr Pearl – as renowned for his own tiny 18-inch waist as he is for the designers with whom he has collaborated, including Christian Lacroix and Thierry Mugler – was also at the fitting. One of his beautiful corsets was to provide the basis of the dress.

Victoria liked Vera right from the start. "To look at her, she's very, very small, she's very, very skinny and you'd think she was very shy, but she's not," says Victoria. "She's quite over the top really. She was a very family oriented person, too – which I think is lovely – and she was really pleased to be doing this. It's an exciting time when you're planning a wedding and it was nice to have people who are excited about it, as well. I've had certain designers before now who thought they were too cool – and I hate that attitude. I've had run-ins with certain designers whose attitude seems to be, 'I don't like people wearing my clothes.' Well, if you don't like people wearing your clothes, why the bloody hell do you make clothes?"

Victoria had a strong idea of what she wanted: sexy but not obvious. "Sexy in a kind of virginal way," as she puts it. She was also well aware of what people were expecting her to wear – "a tight little number with a great big slit up the side." In the event it was a £50,000 champagne coloured affair, made up of a fitted strapless bodice with a zip at the back and a full A-line skirt made of Clerici Duchess satin, the finest Italian satin in the world. Underneath the skirt, Victoria wore a petticoat made from 50 metres of tulle, which had been stiffened with horse hair and underneath the bodice she wore a corset made by Mr Pearl. An Italian mill had dyed the dress to Victoria's specifications.

The result was a publicity coup for both Vera and Victoria, not least because Victoria was the first British celebrity to wear a Vera Wang wedding dress. "It was a fairy princess dress, the shape of the gown drew attention to her small waist," says Laura O'Brien, Vera Wang's public relations director. "Vera only makes six to ten couture wedding dresses a year and has six to eight people working on each one. Victoria's

The most famous woman in the world. Pictures of Victoria such as this have appeared in practically every major newspaper and magazine around the world.

Does my bum look big in this? Victoria and Geri during the filming of *Spiceworld*.

Top: Early days for Britain's most famous couple. David and Victoria are pictured here outside David's house in Manchester in 1997.
Bottom left: Victoria's husband is one of the finest footballers in the world. Here he is spotted with Alex Ferguson, celebrating Manchester United's defeat of Newcastle United in the 1999 FA Cup.
Bottom right: It didn't take long for Posh 'n' Becks to become, not only faces recognised across the world, but also genuine fashion icons. Here they announce their engagement to the world. Notice the rings!

David and Victoria's love for each other blossomed into the wedding of the century. It was held at the luxurious Luttrellstown Castle (*top*). The couple are seen here on the famous thrones they had at the wedding (*bottom left*); and the pictures were sold for a cool £1 million (*bottom right*).

Perhaps the most high-profile guest at the wedding was superstar baby Brooklyn! This is the first ever picture taken of him, just days after he was born.

David and Victoria's devotion to their son cannot be denied. Although quite what Brooklyn thinks about his Dad's tattoo is another question...

Victoria is known to be very generous towards her family. (*Top*) Louise and Christian Adams with the new cars bought for them by their famous sister. (*Bottom*) The Adams Family, from right to left, Dad Tony, Mum Jackie, Sister Louise, Brother Christian, and Christian's girlfriend Lucy.

Victoria Beckham is a girl who can truly be said to have made her dreams come true…

own dress took two preliminary consultations, six fittings in New York and London and 15 months to make."

For her wedding shoes, Victoria wore cream, high-heeled satin sandals with a 10-centimetre heel – a prototype for Vera's new autumn collection – and on her head, she wore a gold and diamond coronet made by Slim Barrett. Her "something old" was the crucifix David had given her for Christmas the previous year – "I've never actually worn it. I've been saving it for the wedding," said Victoria. Her "something borrowed" was a brooch pinned inside the dress that her mother and grandmother had also worn on their wedding days, the "something new" was the dress itself and the "something blue" was taken care of by antique blue taffeta bows sewn into the dress.

Of course, both the bride and the groom were dripping with jewellery, apart from the crucifix and tiara. David and Victoria both love jewels and for their wedding, they had rings designed and made by Asprey and Garrard. Victoria's ring featured a Marquise-cut diamond supported by three grain set baguette diamonds on either side and set in 18-carat yellow gold. David wore an eternity ring with 24 baguette diamonds and 24 smaller ones, also in 18-carat yellow gold. That wasn't all. David's wedding present to Victoria was a pair of emerald cut diamond earrings in 18-carat gold to match her wedding ring along with an 18-carat gold waist chain with a diamond at one end, all from Asprey and Garrard (although she didn't actually wear all of it on the day itself – moderation in all things). Victoria's present to him was a Breguet steel wristwatch and David was also wearing a diamond Cartier bracelet, which Victoria had bought him the previous year. Victoria's bouquet followed the woodland theme: it was a selection of green berries, twigs, blackberries and brambles.

David is a natural dandy, and so it was inevitable he'd make something of a splash with his own outfit, as well. His cream suit was designed by Timothy Everett, who also dresses Tom Cruise, and it comprised a knee length cream jacket over cream trousers, with a gold and cream waistcoat, cream shirt and cravat, cream top hat and cream shoes by Manolo Blahnik.

David's team mate Gary Neville, who had been with David when David saw Victoria for the first time in the video for *Say You'll Be There*, was the best man. The bridesmaids were Victoria's sister Louise, who was 22 at the time, Louise's daughter Liberty, then 13 months and David's niece Georgina, 16 months. Louise wore a dress by Chloe, then Stella McCartney's label, which was made up of a fitted cream corset, laced at the back and decorated with copper and gold flowers and diamonds and a long cream bias-cut skirt.

The two little girls were dressed as flower fairies. Their outfits were made by the theatrical costumiers Angels & Bermans: they were wearing little cream dresses with gossamer wings and wreaths of fake ivy were wrapped around their wrists and ankles. They had tiny coronets of ivy and twigs, which they wore on their head. David and Victoria had given all three bridesmaids £8,000 diamond necklaces from Tiffany: Gary Neville received a £12,000 Cartier watch with a special engraving, while Victoria's brother Christian, who was an usher, was given a £12,000 gold and silver Rolex watch.

The obligatory wedding crisis had actually happened the previous day: Sir Elton John, no less, had been due to play at the wedding, but had had to cancel at the last minute. "The day before the wedding, as they were in the drawing room of the castle posing for pictures with Brooklyn, Victoria got a phone call on her mobile," says a friend who was there. "It was David Furnish [Elton John's partner] saying that Elton had been taken to hospital with a heart scare – and there was no way he would be able to make it to the wedding.

"David and Victoria were genuinely upset. They were really, really concerned for him. He was going to play for them at the wedding, and they were very excited about that. But when that phone call came it wasn't disappointment that they felt – it was horror. That spoiled the mood for the whole of the Saturday afternoon.

But it showed – in the middle of this fairytale
wedding – that they were genuinely human.
They even spent part of their honeymoon in
France, where he was recuperating, so they
could visit him. It was very sweet."

The day itself, however, went according to
plan. Victoria spent the morning getting ready:
she had her make-up artist, her hairdresser and
her stylist to hand, while David did likewise
elsewhere in the castle. The wedding itself
began when close family members began to
gather in the entrance hall of the castle at
around 3pm. They had been staying in the castle
for the previous few days, watching as a
transformation took place. Carpets were
brushed and colossal floral arrangements were
assembled in the major rooms: fresh apples had
been sewn into an ivy arrangement along the
master staircase and pierced to release their
scent. The vast marquee was connected to the
castle by means of a leafy walkway, which
stretched across the lawns from the French
windows of the library. Created by Simon
Lycett, the walkway was decorated with a

swathe of birch trees and Irish reeds had been woven into mats to make a thatched covering. Lights were entwined into it and ivy finished off the decoration.

Even those family members who had been party to the planning were overawed. "I still can't believe it," David's mother Sandra, who was wearing a white Frank Usher suit, said at the time. "All these things we've talked about for months are actually here." Her husband was no less impressed. "It's just something special – a fairy tale," he said. "Victoria's an absolutely lovely girl and I feel very, very proud of the two of them." A bonus came when Ted met one of the guests – Sir Bobby Charlton, who was there with his wife Norma. "He was my absolute hero when I was a youngster," said Ted, "and my favourite moment was when I finally got to meet him alongside David. He was everything I imagined he would be – and a bit more."

Victoria's father Tony was similarly overcome. "When I went into the marquee with Victoria earlier," he said on the day, "the orchestra was rehearsing *Goodbye* (the Spice

Girl's Christmas hit, which had been specially reworked for the occasion) and I got so emotional that we had to have a bit of a cuddle. In fact, I got so emotional that I had to take a bike out and cycle round the golf course to get over it. I didn't think I would ever be emotional. I can be as hard as nails at times, but today – I mean this whole thing has been on the drawing board for so long and to see it coming together is very, very moving."

The wedding itself was held in the little folly chapel, covered in ivy. It was perched above a stream about 500 metres from the castle itself. "The folly was a ruin and very cave-like when we found it, but Victoria loved the look of it," says Peregrine. "We had to do a lot of work to get it ready for the day – we had to bring builders in, put up scaffolding, lay a new floor and install power."

"There isn't a church on the estate, so we had to find a location on the premises that we could get licensed for a wedding ceremony," adds Victoria. "We were just driving and we found the folly, which was in a complete state – a hermit had been living there. It was overgrown, half the floor was missing, and there were big holes in the walls – it was just like walking into a garden shed. But we just looked at each other and thought, 'This is the place.' It was just big enough for our closest family and friends. I wanted the ceremony to be as private as possible."

Only 29 guests were invited to see the wedding ceremony itself. These guests included the other three remaining Spice Girls as well as Mel B's husband Jimmy Gulzar and daughter Phoenix Chi. Mel was wearing a floor length black dress with spaghetti straps, Emma was in a miniskirt, waistcoat, long morning coat and homburg hat, all in white and designed by Copperwheat Blundell, along with high-heeled sandals by Gina and Mel C was also in white, in her case trousers, a Daryl K white sleeveless top and trainers.

Shortly before the ceremony began, guests were collected from the castle by a fleet of Mercedes, also decorated in flower and apple arrangements and taken on a five-minute drive to the folly. The 38-year old Bishop of Cork, the Right Reverend Paul Colton was officiating at the ceremony as he was rector of the parish. He had met the couple at the end of the previous year. "I didn't see the ceremony as a marriage between two celebrities, but of a couple who are very much in love," he says. "They had the same preparation and consultations as any other couple I have ever married."

The bishop was, however, delighted to be marrying the couple for reasons of his own. "The priest who married them was a huge Manchester United fan and was wearing Man U socks during the ceremony," says one friend who was present. "He got a real buzz out of marrying David, and also that there were so many Manchester United players in the church."

The couple set out: first David, accompanied by Gary and driving a £230,000 silver convertible Bentley Azure. Then Victoria: after her stylist Kenny Ho had made final adjustments to her dress and make-up artist Karin Darnell touched up her face, she walked down the purple carpet, which had been laid onto the castle's steps, and took her place in a silver Bentley Arnage. Arriving at the castle, Victoria was greeted by a trumpet fanfare, played by pageanters, who were dressed in traditional Irish costume and waiting on the roof. The steps up to the chapel had also been draped with ivy.

Inside, a string quartet, which had been entertaining guests swung into the traditional wedding march from Wagner's *Lohengrin*. Victoria took her father's arm and approached the altar where David and Brooklyn – dressed all in cream – were waiting for her. The ceremony began: during the reading by Reverend Lynda Peilow – "As the father has loved me, so I have loved you; abide in my love" – David leaned over and planted a kiss on Victoria's shoulder. The Right Reverend Colton then began his address: "David and Victoria, Victoria and David – the marriage service doesn't give us a way of putting these names in order – but through your whole married life you put each other first."

He went on to comment on the beauty of the ceremony (apart from the noise of the helicopters above) and continued, "Why do we do this? Why do we make everything so beautiful? It's simply because words fail us at a time like this. So we do all these beautiful things because they say better than words can, 'Thank you' and 'I love you.' There is a lot of interest in this marriage and we are all excited to be here. But what matters is in David's heart and what is in Victoria's."

Reverend Colton then went on to warn the couple about temptation, quoting an old Irish priest: "The eyes that over cocktails seem so very sweet, may not seem so amorous over Shredded Wheat." He went on to say that there were three ingredients in a happy marriage: good communication, caring for other people and "finding a place for spirituality and God in your lives." Then the service proper commenced – Victoria did not promise to obey – and, to whoops of joy and handclapping from the congregation, at 4.49pm, David and Victoria were declared man and wife. Prayers were said as David and Victoria knelt at the altar. "Almighty God, giver of life and love, bless Victoria and David who you have now joined together in marriage. Give them wisdom and devotion in their life together, that each may be to the other a strength in need, a comfort in sorrow and a companion in joy. Mendelssohn's *Wedding March* began and the deed was done. The couple were married.

And now the fun began. Back at the castle, the remainder of the 226 guests walked up the purple carpeted steps to be greeted with a 15-feet tall column bursting with a floral arrangement of red roses and purple flowers. More pageanters in Irish dress were on the battlements playing a fanfare, while six foot silk flames burst out of the turret. A purple flag, featuring David and Victoria's crest fluttered in the breeze. Inside, a pianist played while guests sipped champagne and nibbled on canapés. The atmosphere was very emotional. "It was very lovely," said Louise Adams. "I think everybody there was in tears," says David's sister Joanne. "It was so emotional. All of us were in tears, including Victoria and David."

At 6.45pm, David and Victoria made an entrance down the castle's main staircase – to the sound of *Beauty and the Beast* as both are great Disney fans – and made their way towards the marquee and the reception. The marquee was carpeted in red, while the walls were covered with a pleated ivory taffeta lining. The flower arrangements continued the Robin Hood theme: they were done in burgundy, green and purple. The tables were covered in dark green velvet overlaid with cream coloured Irish calico and trimmed with purple velvet. "It was a Robin Hood look meets Conran," says Simon Lycett. "Between us all we discussed every detail possible. One of Victoria's own ideas was to cover a wall with birch trees and different foliages to make it look like the waiters were coming out of a forest. This was in keeping with the natural look David and Victoria wanted to achieve."

Halfway through the evening, David and Victoria affected a costume change. Victoria donned an outfit by Antonio Beradi, and it was much closer to what some people expected the wedding dress to be: a strapless, fishtail gown of purple satin split up to the thigh and lined with red silk. She had a wreath of hand-made silk flowers over one shoulder and wore strappy silver Manolo Blahnik sandals. David and Brooklyn wore matching attire: David sported a double breasted purple jacket with red silk lining, purple trousers and purple waistcoat, while Brooklyn had on a purple version of what he had been wearing earlier. The boys' clothes were also designed by Beradi. David had also had his hair put into a quiff and was sporting purple suede shows from Manolo Blahnik.

The table decorations, which were made up of candles, greenery and apples, followed the theme through. Moss-coloured candles were dotted about, there were two huge chandeliers that were also decorated with foliage, apples and sparkling lights. There were 10-foot-high Georgian-style glass windows built into the marquee, draped with cream-coloured voiles. The bride and groom sat in their own private alcove, which was lined with green Irish velvet. More pertinently, perhaps, they were seated on thrones – actually, antique Austrian chairs worth £9,000 each. Nearby Brooklyn sat in his favourite swinging chair, which had been decorated in burgundy velvet with gold ribbons.

An 18-piece string orchestra played in the background as guests tucked into the dinner that was prepared by chef Jason Reynolds. Victoria had said she wanted plain rather than "fiddled with" food and so the menu was as follows: roasted red pepper and tomato soup served in hollowed out pumpkins, chicken with asparagus, roast potatoes and a French bean and sugar snap pea medley and a herb jus. There was deep fried Irish brie with cranberry sauce for vegetarians and pudding was a choice between sticky toffee pudding and summer berry terrine.

At 10.30pm, it was time to cut the cake. It was a three-tiered cake: one tier was fruit cake, one was vanilla sponge and one was carrot cake. The cake was also decorated in keeping with everything else: smothered in green and purple leaves made of icing, with the tiers held up with pillars made of apples. At the top was a fondant sculpture of a naked David and Victoria. The couple cut the cake with a specially made Wilkinson sword: it was a present from

Brooklyn and had been engraved with their crest
and an inscription.

Afterwards came the speeches. "Ladies and
gentleman many people would like to be here
today, but it is you David and Victoria have
chosen," Tony began, perhaps forgetting that at
a wedding the guests honour the bride and
groom with their presence, not vice versa. "It is
with great pride that I speak to you for a few
moments about our bride and groom. Obviously
it is very difficult for me to find anything to say
that hasn't already been written by the News of
the World, The Sun, the Daily Mirror ... need I
go on?" Victoria, said Tony, had never been any
trouble.

"She started dance classes at the age of three
and was soon rushing home from school to
change from her uniform to a leotard to kick her
legs about. Little did she know that a few miles
away there was a little boy changing from his
uniform into shorts to kick a ball around. They
continued with enthusiasm and at 16 both left
home to continue their training. Victoria went
to dance college in Epsom and we all know

where David went. As it happened, they both did quite well!"

The speech continued with the usual joviality to be found on these occasions. David, said Tony, had seen a member of an all-girl band on television and pointed her out as the woman he would marry. "Unfortunately," said Tony, "he was talking about Louise from Eternal and Jamie Redknapp got there first." He then went on to relate the real story about the meeting and ended up with saying, "This afternoon I have given David someone who is very precious to me, but I know he will look after her, as he always does, with utmost love and affection. We know we couldn't wish for a better son-in-law." And with that, he toasted the bride and groom.

Then it was David's turn. "Thank you, Tony, for that speech – it means more to us than you will ever know," he began. "My wife and I" – there was a huge cheer at this – "would like to thank you for coming. I'm sure you'll all agree that the bridesmaids looked absolutely beautiful and stunning and I'd like to say that our mums have scrubbed up very well today, too. No seriously, they look stunning. What can I say? My mother and father-in-law have loved and supported me and been there for me and obviously that means the world to me. I will love and look after Victoria and treat her like a princess – which she always wants to be treated like."

He went on to pay tribute to his new brother and sister-in-laws, his own family, Gary; and spoke of his love for Brooklyn. He also showed that confidence in his own sexuality which makes it easy for him to joke about his image as a gay icon: "I'd like to say that I really love you Gary and you'll notice that we kiss a lot on the pitch!"

Finally Gary stood up to speak, wrapped in a curtain in homage to David's sarong. "He speaks well that Julian Clarey, doesn't he?" Gary remarked. There were the jokes, the reading out of the telegrams – including one from Sir Alex Ferguson, who had been unable to attend as he was at another wedding that day and a joke telegram from David's nemisis Diego Simeone, in the form of a red card. People are always asking me why I kiss David Beckham," Gary went on, also able to poke fun at himself in a most unfootballerish way. "My answer is that I'd usually do much more than that to a six foot blond in shorts with legs up to the armpits."

After coffee and petit fours, along with lots more wine, David and Victoria led the guests into a second room in the marquee, this one decorated in Moroccan style. It had purple and gold drapes, huge gold statues holding up flower arrangements and a sunken dancefloor painted in black and white chequerboard design. Dotted about were chaise longues and leopard print cushions, with low level tables bearing dishes of sweet bonbons.

Dancing began – the DJ was Hugo Fuller – and at 2am, guests gathered on a huge balcony built into one side of the marquee. It was decorated in black, with a drinks bar covered in zebra skin, on top of which perched a huge Egyptian-style cat sculpture. From here, they could watch the final act of the wedding celebrations – a four and a half minute firework display. And from there, the guests retired to bed.

Victoria defends herself against claims that the wedding was just a little ostentatious. "Whatever we do, we know we're going to get criticised," she says. "Some people will say it was over the top. But if we'd had a small wedding, they would have said, 'Couldn't they have done something bigger?' We don't care what people say – as long as we're happy and our families are happy, that's all that matters."

And for those who think it was a little over the top, the happy couple were surprisingly down to earth when it came to wedding gifts. They asked for Marks & Spencer vouchers or Selfridges vouchers – or asked guests to make donations to The Meningitis Trust.

Strangely enough, one rumour was to circulate about the wedding that could not have been further from the truth: namely, that David had had too much to drink to consummate the marriage that night. "That is not true," says Victoria forcefully. "We weren't actually that drunk. We'd had a few but I didn't want to get so drunk that I couldn't remember anything. You wouldn't want to be throwing up on your wedding night, would you? No, David was fine, absolutely fine."

As it happens, Victoria was being disingenuous. According to a very close friend, the couple, unlike the guests, were stone cold sober. But David's duties that night were of quite a different order: before he and Victoria could get on with making whoopee, they had to spend the remainder of the night choosing which pictures to release to publicise the occasion. It was hard work – but that's showbiz.

Shhhhh!

10

Clouds on the Horizon

The honeymoon was brief. Victoria and David had wanted to spend it on an island in the Indian Ocean, but Sir Alex Ferguson wouldn't give David the time off, and so, accompanied by Brooklyn, they spent four days in the South of France at Sir Andrew Lloyd Webber's villa in Cap Ferrat. Victoria was seething. "I don't want to say too much but it was sad we had to leave early," she says pointedly. "David doesn't get a lot of time off. He works so hard. But, after all, it is his job." And it would appear she has still not entirely forgiven Sir Alex to this day. "You do think, 'Oh, I want a honeymoon,'" she says. "It can be upsetting. But his commitment to his footballers is phenomenal. I know to a certain extent David feels he's a sort of father figure." So, on their return, they moved in with Victoria's parents – when David was not living in the flat in Alderley Edge – and it was straight back to business, not least as Victoria set about carving out a solo career.

The Spice Girls were still together and about to return to the studios to record a new album. The other three girls, though, had all done solo projects and now it was Victoria's turn. But what should that solo project be? To paraphrase John Lennon's remarks about Ringo's drumming, not only is Victoria's singing not the best in Britain, it's not even the best in the Spice Girls. So what was to come next? As it happened, putative actress and talkshow hostess were both on the cards – but, above all, of course, there was the serious business of getting on with being one half of Posh and Becks.

First, though, there was some personal business to attend to and that was rumoured to be a breast enhancement operation at London's Wellington Hospital that September, at a cost of £10,000. Victoria has always steadfastly denied it: – "I haven't had a boob job," she says. "If I had, I'd have had them done bigger than this." However, the fact of the matter is that as the rest of her has got smaller – Victoria is now a size six – her breasts have got larger. Nature does not usually work that way and while wonderbras can be a help, they can't create something out of nothing. Insiders who have watched her over the last few years believe that not only has she had at least two breast enhancement operations, she's had other cosmetic work done, too.

"Victoria's view is that the surgery is nobody's business but her own," says a friend. "She's always denied it but yes, she has had work done on her bust. Her nose has also been slimmed down a bit too – she used to think it was bulbous. She's also had her teeth fixed."

Victoria's changing shape can be put down to something else, too. She seems to keep changing the size and status of the implants. "If you look at the photographs that came out from Mel B's party early this year, you can see that she'd had the implants taken out again," says the friend. "As far as I know, she's had them put in, taken out and put back in. That was all done because she's so health conscious."

For Posh and Becks, life was not running altogether smoothly. There was trouble from the in-laws as David's Uncle Peter – who was not invited to the wedding – spoke out against Victoria, saying that the nuptials were vulgar and that David had changed for the worse since he'd met her. "That lavish display didn't fit in with what I know of David," he says. "It was rather extravagant and over the top: the word tacky springs to mind. But it's probably Victoria's influence, not David."

Then Victoria was voted to be Britain's least-admired celebrity in a national opinion poll. Victoria fought back. "I never asked anyone to look upon me as a role model," she sniffed, before hitting the shops once again.

There were compensations: Victoria became the first woman to have two waxworks of her on display at Madame Tussauds at the same time, one of her in the Spice Girls and one with her famous husband. Next, a newspaper tracked down the thrones the couple had been seated on at their wedding and handed them over as a present. "I love being married," crowed Victoria, before announcing that she had changed her name from Adams to Beckham.

It seemed to suit both of them. Victoria revealed that the ever protective David started every day by making her a packed lunch and filling her car with petrol although "in a year he'll probably be lying in bed, going, 'Sod off, make your own lunch.'" And it emerged that she was quite as protective of David as he of her: "We were at this wedding and sat with Dennis [Wise] and his girlfriend and I said, 'Dennis, are you a bully when you play?' He said, 'I can be.' I said, 'If you ever kick my husband I will come and kick you.' And I would." What David felt about his wife defending his honour in public was not revealed.

Victoria was developing a habit of putting her foot in it, in fact, especially given that David had to face Manchester United fans every Saturday. These fans do not easily forgive and forget. Earlier in the year, after giving birth, she announced that both Brooklyn and David were breast feeding and later had to explain that what she *actually* meant was that she was expressing milk so that David could feed it to Brooklyn later. But the damage was done and David had to put up with some taunts on the subject. Now, in an interview for *Vanity Fair*, she insisted that, contrary to popular belief, David was extremely intelligent. Then she ruined it all by saying how devastated she was when he beat her at Trivial Pursuit. "I was devastated because I got beaten by David Beckham!" She added salt to the wound with her breathless justification of it. David, apparently, got really easy questions, Victoria explained and she got really hard ones.

This, of course, was just a foretaste of what would happen when, in the following January, she revealed and subsequently denied that David wears her underwear – "Becks Wears My Kecks!" screamed the headlines. "Least said, soonest mended," is a motto she might like to bear in mind. As for Kecksgate itself, the repercussions abound to this day. "No, he doesn't still wear my knickers," Victoria snaps.

"Actually, he never did. What happened was this woman said to me during a live interview, 'So, do you dress your husband like that for a joke or does he choose to dress like that?' Of course the audience laughed and so I replied, 'If you think that's funny, you should see what he's got on underneath. He's go my knickers on!' But it was just a joke. I mean, you'd only have to put the two of us next to each other to know he couldn't fit one of his legs in my knickers, for goodness sake." Beckham himself then denied it to no less august a person than Michael Parkinson on the latter's chat show, gently pointing out that he is quite a bit bigger than Victoria. Even so, Victoria still does not seem to have learned the wisdom of maintaining silence worthy of a Trappist monk when it comes to sensitive issues and her husband.

There was also the matter of buying a house. The couple were commuting between Goff's Oak and their penthouse flat in Alderley Edge, but Victoria was never really happy living up in the North West and so a proper base down south was needed. It was thus that they came across "Beckingham Palace." The house, a mock Georgian-style construct in Sawbridgeworth on the border of Hertfordshire and Essex, was built in the 1930s. Previously a council-owned property for disabled children, before being bought by a property developer, it had been empty for the previous nine years and had an indoor swimming pool, seven bedrooms, a two-bedroom apartment for staff and a large entrance hall with a chandelier.

Although it would be eighteen months before they moved in, the Beckhams had found their dream home. Most importantly for the privacy conscious couple, it was in a secluded spot, accessible only by a private drive and set in 24 acres. The price was £2.5 million and it was a short drive away from Victoria's parents, but not everyone was happy about the couple moving in. "They are the kind of people one would dread as neighbours," sniffed the late Dame Barbara Cartland, who at the time lived nearby.

"They have lots of money but no class and no idea how to behave. Heaven knows the sort of people they will attract."

Dame Barbara was not alone in her criticism of the couple. There were fears that David was partying too much at the expense of his football: on one notorious occasion, he was spotted sporting a bandana at the launch of Jade Jagger's jewellery collection. Sir Alex Ferguson was not pleased and docked David two weeks wages: £50,000. It escaped no one's notice that had he not been wearing the bandana (Victoria's doing, sniffed the detractors), he would probably not have been photographed, Sir Alex wouldn't have found out and all would have been well.

Victoria seemed to have far too great a say in his life, choosing clothes for him and getting him to dress in his 'n' hers outfits, although ironically enough, the one area in which David was prepared to stand firm was the matter of his career. Victoria wanted him to leave Manchester United and sign up with a club down south, which would mean she would be closer to her family and to London: David refused. "I did all I could to try to get David to leave Manchester," she said at the time. "I've tried to get through to him how desperately I miss my family and friends down in London." And when David re-signed with United, she commented, "I was a bit hurt because I was hoping deep down he'd sign for a London club."

The tensions persist to this day. Victoria went on to put her foot in it a couple of months later, both by publicly demanding that David be given a pay rise – £25,000 a week is not enough, she explained – and by saying that one day, he would almost certainly play for another team abroad. But that was as nothing compared to a recent interview she gave to Jerry Springer. Asked which she would save from drowning, Geri Halliwell or Sir Alex, Victoria announced, "I'd let them both drown," before hastily backing down and claiming it was all a joke.

And then there were fears for Brooklyn's safety: with their joint fortune by this time estimated at £25 million (it has grown since then), Victoria and David were worried that he might become a kidnap target, especially after a terrifying episode in which someone tried to grab Brooklyn as the couple were leaving Harrods towards the end of 1999.

It was David who was carrying the child at the time: the man, thought to be a United fan, rushed up and grabbed Brooklyn by the arm. "I just want a picture of me and Brooklyn together, please, please let me," he yelled, at which a horrified and frightened Victoria lashed out and left him sprawling on the ground. "I gave him a massive push and we got into the car quickly," says Victoria. "It was horrible but I did what any mother would do. David and I were both shocked by the whole incident. I was defending my baby and I didn't want anything to happen to him. I feared for Brooklyn's life and just didn't know what was going on." She was very shaken, but still, ever the professional, managed to perform with the rest of the girls in Earls Court, London, that evening.

That is one version of the story, at any rate. Some months later, it was claimed that no such incident had ever happened and that the couple had made the whole thing up in order to get Beckham off a driving ban. Certainly it is the case that in December 1999, David had been banned for eight months for speeding – he was caught driving at 76 mph in a 50 mph zone in Stockport, Greater Manchester in July 1999 – and appealed, saying that he was being chased by the paparazzi and was worried about his safety. The car he claimed was chasing him has never been traced.

The Harrods story came out during that appeal, as Beckham was describing to the judge the kind of pressure he lived under. "Me and my wife was in Harrods shopping and as we came out we noticed there was 10 to 15 photographers outside the store," he said. "I was going out holding Brooklyn, my wife was in front and as we were going out someone lunged towards Brooklyn and me and my wife pushed them off and we got in the back of the car."

Some commentators simply did not believe the Beckhams' tale. "Strangely, the interview was not captured on film either by the CCTV cameras outside Harrods or by the dozen or so photographers within inches of their Mercedes," writes Andrew Morton in his book about the couple. "A housewife quoted as a witness has also proved untraceable." Michael Mann, a Harrods media relation officer agrees. "No one saw it, not the doormen and not the photographers," he says. "In my opinion it may not have happened and was possibly for the papers."

David and Victoria were furious at suggestions that they had made the whole thing up and their agent issued a statement on their behalf. "Victoria and David Beckham strongly refute suggestions that an incident involving Brooklyn outside Harrods was in any way made up or fabricated," it read. "They are disappointed that these and various other allegations have been given any credence. The book [by Morton] does not actually claim that the incident did not happen but simply reports that some people do not believe it." Whatever the truth of it, it had a happy ending – David's driving ban was overturned.

And there is no doubting the fact that the couple were genuinely extremely concerned about their son. To protect Brooklyn, David and Victoria hired two security guards but even that wasn't enough to satisfy their fears: David started taking him along to training. "I want to check that Brooklyn is OK all the time," says Victoria anxiously. "I can't help myself." This was no idle paranoia; as well as the Harrods incident and hate mail, David had even been sent a bullet through the post with his name on it.

These fears took on a much more worrying angle the following year. In January 2000 details emerged of a plot to kidnap Victoria and Brooklyn. The plan had been hatched the previous year and centred on November's Euro 2000 qualifier: when David was away at Wembley playing with England against Scotland, Victoria and her son were to be snatched by a three man team and held at an address on Bishop's Avenue, North London, where a £1 million ransom demand would be made. They would then be taken to Wales.

The details of the plot emerged when the owner of the Manchester boutique Flannels, who is a friend of Victoria's, received news of it in a telephone call. She alerted the both the Beckhams and the police and the threat was soon discovered to be real: Victoria and Brooklyn were moved to a safe house and security was improved at their flat in Alderley Edge and the mansion in Hertfordshire. Victoria's parents were also advised to take similar precautions in Goff's Oak.

A senior policeman had contacted the couple's spokesman Alan Edwards with details of the plot the previous October. "He said he was taking what they perceived to be an already established plan to kidnap Brooklyn and Victoria so seriously that they were assigning a top officer," says. Alan. In the event the gang found out that they were under surveillance and shelved the plot: no arrests were made as no written evidence of the plot was discovered. But it had a profound effect on the couple, who have been ever more security conscious since then and who have now fortified Beckingham Palace against intrusion on all sides.

There were other problems, as well. Rumours about Victoria's eating habits were surfacing again, as she became thinner and thinner still. "Victoria has always been obsessed with her figure," says a friend. "After she met David, she was always at the gym. She is always picky over her food. She will not eat anything with oil in it. She gets David to taste her food and if it has oil or butter it goes back. She was worried about losing her figure after Brooklyn was born, but it has gone too far and it bothers David and causes rows."

There were other tensions on the home front, as well. David's parents were reputedly unhappy about his growing closeness to Jackie and Tony Adams, as well as being concerned about the couple's increasingly showbiz lifestyle. Like Sir Alex Ferguson, they were worried it would interfere with David's football and came to a head around the time of the marriage. After the wedding, Ted had confided to a friend, "I just didn't feel part of it." This might have had something to do with the difference between the two families: Victoria' parents were well-off and middle class, David's were not well-off and working class.

"They feel that they have become sidelined as David spends more and more time at the Adams's," said a friend at the time. "Even at the wedding, his speech constantly referred to how much he loved Jackie and Tony and how they had always been there for him. David loves Ted and Sandra and his sisters Lynne and Joanne, but they came second in his speech, which made a lot of people realise just how much Jackie and Tony influence him."

"The simple fact is that they are very different," says a friend. "Victoria's parents, Tony and Jackie, are successful, self-made people who enjoy all the trappings. David's parents, Ted and Sandra, are more ordinary and in touch with their roots." Nowhere was this more in evidence than when the two sets of families turned up to watch David play. "While David's family sit with the ordinary fans and mingle happily, Victoria's prefer to have a private box."

Victoria didn't help matters when David's sister Lynne got married in October 1999: she didn't turn up to the wedding. It could hardly have been more different from her own – Lynne was marrying Colin Every in front of 30 guests at a registry office in Hornchurch, Essex, with a reception afterwards in a local hotel. To make matters even worse, two excuses were offered on Victoria's behalf: first, that she had been up with Brooklyn all night and secondly, that she was recording in Sheffield. Either way, her absence was not the most diplomatic way of handing a slightly fraught situation and did nothing to dispel rumours about tensions between the two families.

Victoria also hadn't sorted out the future direction of her own career. She was still singing with the Spices, but that clearly wasn't going to last forever and her career as a film star was failing to take off: she had read for a part in

Charlie's Angels, but it eventually went to Lucy Liu, of *Ally McB*eal fame, instead. *SpiceWorld: The Movie* might have been entertaining, but it clearly not going to be a springboard to Hollywood stardom.

Christmas approached. Victoria was typically generous in her gifts: a £40,000 white gold and diamond cross from society jeweller Theo Fennell and – allegedly – a £15,000 facelift for her mother. She ruffled feathers yet again, though, when she attended the wedding of Manchester United star Phil Neville to Julie Killilea (although at least she turned up this time.) The invitations asked guests to wear the Man U colours black, red and white, but Victoria had other ideas and turned up in a gold brown antique dress covered in black lace. It was stunning and attention-catching – and it also upstaged the bride. David, incidentally, managed to adhere to the dress code, as did Brooklyn, who was sporting a red bandana. It also later emerged that shortly before the wedding, Victoria had lost the diamond in her engagement ring, a loss that greatly upset her, although she has since replaced it.

Finally, towards the end of the year, life began to go more smoothly again when, still denying rumours of an eating disorder, she had appeared in a very revealing tight leather mini-dress for Sir Elton John's birthday party at The Ivy, which only served to show there was less of her than ever. She co-hosted the Art of Barbie Ball at London's Natural History Museum – a suitable event for a woman who was known to be so devoted to shopping and clothes.

The bash was in aid of the Elton John AIDS foundation and Victoria made an entrance with her co-hosts Sir Elton on one arm and Sir Elton's partner David Furnish on the other. For the occasion, Victoria had donned a pink chiffon gown, which was complemented by Sir Elton's pink sequinned jacket and David's white suit – and David Beckham's pink tie. Becks had flown in specially for the occasion and other guests included Mick Jagger and Jerry Hall, Ruby Wax, Lulu, Claudia Schiffer and Tim

Jeffries. It was a suitably glamorous occasion to banish some of the niggles that had been on the couple's mind.

And the New Year ushered in the next experimental stage in Victoria's career: the television programme *Victoria's Secrets*. Surprisingly entertaining, it had Victoria asking Guy Ritchie about his new relationship with Madonna (he didn't blab), swapping football notes with Vinnie Jones, quizzing *Daily Mirror* editor Piers Morgan about the power of the press ("You have more power than me," he said) and shopping with Sir Elton John who, it transpires, buys three CDs of everything for his three homes in London, Atlanta and the south of France.

Sir Elton asks Victoria what she thinks of Geri Halliwell's new album and Victoria, clearly stunned by the question, freezes. Eventually she manages to change the subject and chats about shopping once more. Relations between the girls had worsened because of a battle between Geri and Emma Bunton to get to Number One in the charts with solo singles: Geri won.

Geri had courted publicity with an energy not even seen when the Spice Girls were still together. She was absolutely everywhere, she may or may not have had a relationship with Chris Evans – the two were seen all over the place together for a week and then spilt abruptly as soon as Geri got to Number One. At the time there was much talk of two redheads getting together, but cynics pointed out that they both had the same public relations man, Matthew Freud. Geri even turned up at *The Sun* newspaper dressed as a schoolgirl, something that Victoria remarked sniffily that she would never do. What Victoria did go on to do, incidentally, when she had a single of her own to promote, was stage a public reunion with David at a branch of Woolworths in Oldham, leading that self same *Sun* to call her "desperate" – but that still lay ahead.

At the time, though, it was an indication of quite how frosty relations had become between Geri and the other Spice Girls, not least because Victoria had been the only one to see her after she left, when she and David had had dinner in the south of France with Geri and George Michael. These dinners would be no more. "Geri thinks Victoria is cold, yes, but Geri's mistaking 'cold' for a lack of interest in Geri Halliwell," says a friend of Victoria. "I don't think Victoria's interested in Geri Halliwell. I don't think Geri inspires much interest in anyone other than herself. Of all the Spice Girls, Geri was the one who was totally wrapped up in herself. It's just Geri objecting to the limelight that is always on Victoria. Everybody knows her face, and David's face. When you are that famous you may appear cold, but only because you're trying to deal with everything that's thrown at you."

Certainly Geri does seem to have become jealous of her old friend. For a start she's dieted down to a similar weight and secondly, the subject of Victoria is taboo in interviews. According to Victoria, Geri copied her [Victoria's] ideas in a recent video, of which more in Chapter 11, and they even seem to compete when it comes to gay mentors. Victoria has Sir Elton and Geri has George

Michael and going solely on the fact that Victoria's mentor has a knighthood and Geri's doesn't, it would appear that Victoria has won.

And, whether she actually cares about her or not, there is now a clear animosity between Victoria and Geri. "I can't stand Geri," Victoria says. "I haven't seen her since a party we were both at a couple of years ago and I'm pleased about that fact. She is one of the most disloyal people I've ever known. When she walked out of the Spice Girls, she almost split up an entire band with her selfish behaviour." The line-up of Persuasion know just how that feels.

Anyway, back to *Victoria's Secrets* – the television programme, that is. Other participants include Ruby Wax, who helpfully explains she only shaves her legs once a year – "When I have my sex" before wrestling with a top she has bought for the occasion under the clothes-conscious eyes of Victoria – Roger Moore and his son Geoffrey, Michael Parkinson and, of course, David Beckham.

Trying to keep a straight face, Victoria starts interviewing her husband before launching herself at him with the words, "I can't do this!" "Victoria," says a patient voice in the background, "that is not very professional." Victoria extricates herself from David's embrace and, with a solemn face, continues the chat. David answers in monosyllables – because, as Victoria explains to the camera, she had told him that makes him very hard to interview.

Victoria managed to land herself in deep water yet again by making a few unguarded remarks in the making of *Victoria's Secrets*, although for once it resulted in public favour swinging in her direction –because the object of her tactlessness was the model Naomi Campbell, who is famous for her temper tantrums, rather than poor old David. On her way to interview the Italian fashion designer Valentino, Victoria announces that she is going to ask if Naomi is a "complete cow," and a "bitch", as Victoria has always found her to be. In the event she lost her nerve when talking to the designer himself being at first more interested in his curtains. But even the few remarks she did make caused an absolute furore. It emerged that Victoria had not been Naomi's greatest fan since an occasion on which the supermodel approached the singer at a party and asked, "Why exactly do they call you Posh?"

"That's rich, coming from you," snapped Posh. Open warfare broke out although Victoria has since said they've patched up their differences, and in the event, when the remarks were made public, it was only Naomi's mother Valerie who stood up for her. Naomi was only being interested, protested Valerie unconvincingly. "Clearly Victoria took offence," she says, "but Naomi was saying to me after the *Victoria's Secrets* show that whether it had been Scary, Baby or Sporty she would have asked the same thing. Naomi just wanted to know how they chose their names. Naomi didn't mean it in an offensive way."

No one was even remotely convinced. Naomi Campbell has a reputation for being even more tactless than Victoria herself, on top of which she is said to possess an absolutely foul temper.

Rather unwisely, Valerie continued, "I know Victoria was offended and I also think she is jealous. In my view, Victoria can't sing and she can't dance. She should go on her bended knees and thank the good God above for letting her make some money, because the girl is talentless. I mean, she's the only one not to have the guts to do solo stuff [this was early 2000] because she knows she is crap. Naomi isn't bothered by Victoria's remarks and will not be taking any legal action. Victoria is a major-league attention-seeker. She might think she is posh but anyone with any class wouldn't be making comments about her man wearing her undies. The Queen of England wouldn't turn around and say that. It isn't posh.

"I feel sorry for David Beckham. A footballer is supposed to be macho. Everyone is now taking the mickey out of him. Victoria doesn't know when to shut her gob. She is stupid and thick. I sat there watching this show and I simply couldn't believe what I was seeing or hearing. If anyone is a bitch it has to be Victoria – she even humiliated her own poor husband.

Look how Victoria slags off Geri... she's the bitch and everyone should know it."

Victoria didn't respond to Valerie's comments, for once wisely keeping her mouth shut. And anyway, she was about to prove Valerie wrong. For, like the other Spice Girls, she was indeed about to embark on a solo career...

11

Solo Spice

Victoria Beckham has got what she has always wanted: a handsome husband, a beautiful house, a successful career and an adorable child. But that very success has brought problems she had never even dreamed of – not least, how to keep it going? Despite frequent denials from the band's record company, the Spice Girls would appear to be no more, at least for the near future, which means Victoria is facing a more uncertain future than she has at any time since she was a teenager. And the omens are not good.

On September 17, Victoria's second solo single, *Not Such An Innocent Girl*, was released, shortly to be followed by her first album, *Victoria Beckham*. Virgin Records is said to have invested a staggering £1 million on the album and Victoria will be hoping that it and the single do better than her first attempt at solo chart success, which came out last year: *Out Of My Mind*, a collaboration with Dane Bowers and Truesteppers. After a very public battle with Sophie Ellis Bexter, Victoria failed to hit the top slot, and, whether she likes it or not, she can not afford to have that happen again.

There has always been intensive speculation that the Spice Girls as a group were greater than the sum of their parts and this is so far proving to be the case: only Mel C, always regarded as the real talent in the band, has so far achieved genuine solo success. Even Geri, who has the highest profile after Victoria, is more famous for her ever decreasing midriff than she is for anything she has actually sung, and if they are not careful, the girls will find their sing-by date has crept up faster than they were expecting. Victoria, who has always craved fame and is well aware of the perils of celebrity, will be only too conscious of this. Ironically, given the Spice Girls' success when they first started out – the string of number one hits, the astonishing debut in the United States – Victoria is in some ways back where she started. And famous or not, she still has a lot to prove.

Before Victoria got round to releasing her first solo single in the autumn of 2000 there was plenty to keep her occupied. For a start, the designer Maria Grachvogel was responsible for launching Catwalk Spice, when Victoria was persuaded to model the British designer's autumn winter collection for London Fashion Week in February. "I chose Maria because I love her clothes and we get on really well," says Victoria. "I wanted to give her something back after all she has done for me. Maria's great and she puts up with me telling her the split should be higher and the neck-line lower."

The appearance was certainly a publicity coup for both of them. Pictures of Victoria opening the show in lime satin hot pants and an embroidered tank top and then rounding off the proceedings in a split to the thigh plum bustier dress dominated the front pages. Moreover, she took to the catwalk with aplomb, although admitting afterwards that the whole experience had been nerve wracking. But while the fashion crowd spoke admiringly of Victoria's toned legs and year-round tan, other commentators couldn't help but notice how very, very thin Victoria had become...

Her first outing as a model, however (as well as her very public hobby – retail therapy) brought with it an unexpected accolade: in May, she was voted Britain's top shopping icon for her outstanding ability to spend money faster than most other people. (This may also, perhaps, be a clue as to the bond she has formed with Sir Elton John.) Channel 4's *She's Gotta Have It* and readers of *Company* magazine were the judges: they unequivocally put Victoria at the top of the list, with Kate Moss at number two and All Saint Nicole Appleton in third place. "She's the celebrity above all others who has more women rushing to the high street to rip off her stylish look," said Sam Baker, editor of Company. Victoria herself was equivocal. She admitted in an interview shortly before the award, "I still feel quite guilty about spending it. It's hard to justify spending £5,000 on a coat when there are people living rough on the street."

It turned out that there was one person in the family who was even worse than Victoria, though: David. "I saw some old rock 'n' roll T-shirts in Los Angeles which had been customised with sequins," Victoria continued brightly. "They were $250 each, which I thought was far too expensive, so I didn't buy him one. The next day he was in the same shop with my sister and he bought 12."

After the modelling, there then followed something a little more sinister: a warning, if ever there needs to be one, of the perils of celebrity. In April 2000, Victoria and David travelled from Miami to Manchester, via London Heathrow, on British Airways for the first, long leg of the trip before transferring to British Midland to fly up north. Victoria had been away a whole two weeks, she later explained, which is why she had quite as much

luggage as she did – 11 cases for the whole
party, which included her son, her mother, her
sister, her niece and a security guard, only about
eight of them were hers. Four went missing.
Most were Louis Vuitton, worth £700 each and
that was before you even began to think about
the contents. All went well up to leaving
Heathrow: on arrival in Manchester, Victoria
discovered her cases were gone.

Victoria was not pleased. To begin with there
was the minor matter of resolving the situation
with BA: she demanded first class travel for life
by way of compensation (even in moments of
crisis, Victoria maintains her bargaining skill),
and she settled for a reported £100,000.

Then the cases turned up anyway, except in
the farcical manner that events occur on Planet
Celeb, as opposed to the real world. A binman
called Mark Oliver, then 20, from Stanwell in
Surrey, rang Victoria's nail technician
(subsequent acres of press reports explained
that a nail technician deals with false nails, as
opposed to a manicurist, who deals with real
ones) and said that he had stumbled across some

of Victoria's possessions because they'd been dumped in two bin bags at the back of his Ford Transit pick-up.

In these bags he'd discovered a book with the nail technician's number: this he rang and was eventually contacted by Victoria herself, eager to express her gratitude. Oliver told her he'd dumped the bin bags in a rubbish tip. While still talking to her he claimed to make his way to the tip and search for a photograph of baby Brooklyn in a silver frame. He claimed to have found the frame but not the photo and subsequently handed the frame over to Victoria's security guard, Mark Niblett. Oliver said he didn't want a reward: "You won't get one," said Niblett. "She's a bit tight."

Victoria, however, had become suspicious. Oliver, while still on the phone to her, claimed to have climbed a wall and made his way to the dump in less than 30 seconds. The police were called in. Oliver was subsequently arrested on charges of theft: when the police raided his home, they found item's of Victoria's clothing in the wardrobe of Oliver's 16-year old sister

Sadie, including items by Ralph Lauren and Donna Karan. Victoria was summoned to a bizarre identity parade, in which items of clothing were held in front of her to identify. It later emerged that her recovered luggage included two leather boob tubes costing £300 each, £200 Gucci sandals, a £2,000 Dolce & Gabbana suede miniskirt, Versace animal print shoes worth £700, two Patricia Field leather corsets, one red and one black and both costing £400, three Plein Sud jackets in pink, turquoise and purple, several tie-dyed tops, a Maria Grachvogel bikini top with matching sarong – and a great deal more. The total value of the items was £23,000.

In February 2001, Mark Oliver was found guilty of handling stolen goods and sentenced to 15 months in a young offenders' institution. Victoria's mother Jackie Adams described the sentence as "fantastic", but lesser souls couldn't help but point out that by no means all of the clothing had been recovered. Particular attention was paid to Victoria's bikini bottoms – the tops had been recovered but the location of the bottoms was, and still is, a source of mystery...

The subsequent trial, which actually took place in January 2001, provided a priceless glimpse into life *chez* Beckham. Given that she'd been away for a full fortnight, recording with the Spice Girls, Victoria explained that she'd needed to take away practically her entire wardrobe: "There was trousers, skirts, more tops, shoes, handbags – virtually everything I owned," she said at the trial. "I was away for two weeks so I literally took everything. It was virtually all of my clothes." What most upset her, she continued, was the loss of the picture of Brooklyn in its silver frames. It carried an inscription from David saying "Me and Daddy," which was of enormous sentimental significance. Also missing was a baby book with a lock of Brooklyn's hair, a gold embossed book containing lyrics written by Victoria for her solo album and papers which carried details of the Beckhams' business dealings.

The items found in Sadie's wardrobe, a Ralph Lauren denim jacket and a Donna Karan outfit featured in the trial. Given that the Ralph Lauren jacket did not look as posh as its owner was once said to be, Victoria was asked whether Oliver could have mistaken it for something a little cheaper? "A lot of clothes I wear are fashion but are made to look vintage," said Victoria icily. "That is fashion." "It didn't look nothing valuable," Sadie commented. "It's old really, isn't it?" she went on before the case finally reached its halt.

And so it was against this background – modelling, lost luggage, the onerous task of being half of Posh and Becks – that Victoria settled down to the serious business of proving herself to be a serious pop star. It was certainly about time – all the other Spices had set out to make it on their own and so why hadn't she? "It does hit hard if you're told every day you can't sing, you can't dance," Victoria admitted at the time. "And that's what I was being told by the media on a daily basis. I'd had enough of it really. It was David who built up my confidence. I spent a long time thinking about what I would do next. I think the reason this new record is so polished is that we went into the studio with strong ideas."

And so Victoria set out. As ever, she took to the task in hand with all the dedication and focused energy that led her into the Spice Girls. She left no stone unturned, no publicity opportunity missed and, it sometimes seemed, no record shop in the whole of the British Isles unvisited, as she set about doing her stuff. Dane Bowers of Another Level and the dance music outfit Truesteppers were chosen as suitable companions, with Victoria gleefully describing the mix as "Posh and Decks." And she reveals that the single came about through rather unusual circumstances. "I was in the studio with the Spice Girls and Dane was there with the Truesteppers," she says. "He was on his way back from the toilet and we bumped into each other so he asked me to listen to a song. If he hadn't needed a wee wee we would never have done it."

And Victoria lost no time in expressing admiration for her collaborators. "The record was written by Dane in three hours, which was amazing," she said. (With hindsight, that might not have been a wise admission.) "I just put the vocals down as he finished it. It was very quick, but I loved the record. I know Dane and True Steppers have a fan base, but I don't really know who will be mine for my solo material. To be honest, if a thousand people buy the record, I'll be happy."

She was being disingenuous: Victoria wanted a Number One and she set out to get it. Although Victoria might not be the best singer in Britain, she must be one of the most hard-working, given the amount of effort that went into promoting her Spiceless debut: in total, she travelled 8,100 miles in less than two months, gave 67 interviews and performed the song in front of 180,000 people.

Not content with that, David stepped in. If Victoria got to Number One, he announced, he would strip naked and streak around the grounds of Old Trafford. Tragically, that eyestopper was never to be.

And here was a typical day for Victoria: in the run up to the single's release, she managed

10 print interviews, six TV talk shows and a photo shoot on the same day that the video was recorded. She went on to give her first solo performance in Hyde Park's Party in the Park in front of a crowd of 100,000, she played a 1am gig at London's G.A.Y. nightclub – she was introduced to the crowd by her husband – and she had a short stopover in Ibiza. This entailed nightclub appearances, dinner with her record company, television and press conferences – and a bout of food poisoning, which did nothing to put her off her tracks.

Victoria stopped at nothing: she hinted that a very special person can be heard singing on the CD (if you listen very, very closely). "David sings on the single," she said. "You can't really hear him at first, but if you concentrate you can hear him singing the male vocals when Dane sings. He always wanted to sing on a record so Dane and I thought it would be a bit of fun. We all had a great time working on the track, it's been a real family effort."

There were criticisms Victoria was miming to the record: she shrugged them off. "I've been on tour with the Spice Girls singing live at every show and I've just got to the stage where if people think I can't sing then let them think that," she snapped. "I wanted a lot of dancing and you can not dance and sing live like that – something has to go. You look at people like Britney Spears, Janet Jackson and even Michael Jackson and they don't sing live when they are doing such full-on dance routines. People say I sound like a Dalek on this track – well, that's called dance music. It's only old bastards who are writing that and who don't know what dance music is. Most dance music has that sound. I'm criticised every day for doing something or saying something, so now I just do what is important to me."

She gave interviews about everything, including her beauty secrets, which include taking all your make up off before you go to bed and using the face cream Crème de la Mer. (At over £100 a jar, it would have been rather expensive for her fans.) She always uses lip gloss, she confided, before going on to talk about the hair extensions she had had put in at the time – "David prefers my hair long," she announced.

Victoria urged everyone – everyone – to buy her single. On Clyde Radio in Scotland she spoke straight to her target audience – children – telling them what to do. "I've said since day one," she said, "let's have faith in the children out there. There are a lot of great kids who are fans so if you have any pocket money left, help me out."

Not that the original fans of the Spice Girls were left out. Mel C was currently at the top of the charts with *I Turn To You* and Victoria latched onto that. "Mel's at the top today, but we hope to chart a week today and it'd be great if we were Number One," she said. "But we'll just have to wait and see. There's no competition between Mel and I. We're mates and in the same band. If we do it, it'll just mean two different Spice Girls are top of the charts. But I'm not tempting fate, let's just see what happens. We've got a few busy months coming up.

"As well as our solo stuff there's a Spice single and album out in November. It's great doing our own thing, but we all love being in the Spice Girls together. That's how we started, and we want to give something back to our fans, who've been waiting patiently for new Spice Girls material to come out." Mel's thoughts on that one went unrecorded, but she can't have been too pleased at Victoria's efforts, not least because Geri and Emma had also had a very public battle to attain the Number One slot the previous year, a battle that Geri won. As it happened, Mel did lose the Number One slot, but not to Victoria.

And then, of course, there was the "why won't they let me just be me" complaint. "People can be cynical about me, but it won't stop me doing what I want," she said. "I do what I want to do and if people knock it, that's their problem. I'm just being me and loving every minute of it. I'm a Spice Girl, wife and mother. I can't win with some of the people, but I don't care. There's even questions about my weight. I mean, I don't even weigh myself. It's madness. All I want to do right now is establish myself as a solo artist. I've written material for my solo album already and will be going to the studio to master them very soon. I am really excited about the whole thing, and I wouldn't say the whole LP is going to be dance music. It's going to have pop music in it, which I do best. These are exciting times and I'm very lucky to do what I do and I'm enjoying every minute of it."

Then, Victoria stepped into publicity overdrive: appearing on GMTV first thing in the morning, going on to radio interviews for Capital and Kiss FM, then signing sessions on Oxford Street, where David also turned up to give the fans added impetus to clock up those all important sales. David's presence prompted the appearance not only of little girls, but little boys as well, claiming to be there on behalf of their sisters. Nor did their appearance disappoint: Victoria sported a skin tight black leather catsuit, unzipped to show off a large crucifix nestling in her cleavage: David, meanwhile, was in jeans and a mock snakeskin jacket.

It was at this point that Victoria seemed to go too far. The next day she met up with David in a branch of Woolworths in Oldham, in front of 6,000 fans. The pair kissed and cuddled in front of the cameras, bringing the town centre to a standstill, but this did not impress the media: "Desperate!" bellowed one newspaper the following day.

It was all to no avail. In the event Victoria only made it to Number Two, beaten to the top slot by Spiller's *Groovejet* (*If This Ain't Love,*) sung by Sophie Ellis Bextor, then 22 and living in north London. To everyone's delight, Sophie was not only the daughter of former Blue Peter presenter Janet Ellis, but she had attended the private Godolphin and Latymer School in Hammersmith, West London, also the sister school of Hugh Grant's alma mater. The newspapers dubbed it the battle between Posh and Posher, and Sophie certainly played it for all she was worth. For a start, she wandered around in T-shirts emblazoned with "Peckham," a reference to Brooklyn's start in life. "It was a bit cheeky," she said at the time. I saw it in Top Shop a couple of weeks ago and I couldn't resist it."

Sophie then annoyed Victoria even further by making reference to David, when she mused,

"I did consider saying my boyfriend plays for Manchester City, but then I thought better of it." Sophie's mother Janet then weighed into the fray. "Sophie really is posh," she explained helpfully. "She doesn't need a nickname because it's there already." Sophie duly hit the top slot and has done nothing to alleviate the tensions: "I really enjoyed the battle between us, it was good fun," she said brightly in a recent interview. "I'm incredibly passionate about music, that's why I do it and I get excited about the whole thing. I didn't want to do anything that smacked of desperation, you know," she continued, unwisely perhaps, if she really did want to mend fences with Victoria, "because if I did then I would have been letting myself down." And did Victoria enjoy the battle? She was asked. "I don't know what she made of it," said Sophie in a late burst of diplomacy. "I wouldn't presume to put words into her mouth."

Victoria does not forgive and forget. Nearly a year after she pipped Posh to the post, Sophie related how she bumped into Victoria at a television studio and rather unwisely went to say hello: "She had a dressing room two doors down from me and so I thought it would be daft of me not to go in and wish her good luck with everything and just put it to bed," she recounts. "It is quite weird when you do what we do and conversations go back and forth between you in newspapers. I don't think she was surprised when I put my head around the door – she didn't show it if she was. She didn't say anything to me, I suppose there was nothing to say. It was like 'hello' and 'goodbye' from her."

Although she played it down, Sophie was clearly hurt by the incident. "It was just a bit of a bitchy meeting," says a friend of Sophie's. "Sophie probably shouldn't have been surprised, but Victoria basically didn't say a word to her. She didn't even want to look at her, that was the attitude." Nor did Victoria mellow when the two played at Birmingham's Party in the Park in August 2001. She had to use the same dressing room as Sophie – and, incidentally, Geri Halliwell, who was also appearing – causing a logistical nightmare for the organisers, who had to keep them apart. Sophie went on first, followed a little while later by Geri, while Victoria stayed in a nearby hotel room until half an hour before her performance to make doubly sure none of the trio would meet.

The jury is out as to the fate of her second single, but Victoria has once again got a rival to contend with – Kylie Minogue. Kylie's new single *Can't Get You Out Of My Head* is to be released on the very same day as Victoria's CD, which is unfortunate given that Victoria has already postponed her launch date by a week in order to avoid competing with animated pop giant Bob the Builder's new song *Mambo No 5*. Previews of the video have already been released showing Victoria looking thinner than ever and sporting two looks on a sort of modern day Swan Lake theme, in which the two swans, Odette and Odille are white and black and good and evil respectively. One look has Victoria dressed in white with blonde hair (Good Posh), the other has her in vampy black with dark hair (Evil Posh). Victoria's already moaned that Geri Halliwell used the same idea for *her* new video for *Scream If You Wanna Go Faster*, (the video was released before Victoria's but recorded after it). Apparently she is unaware that Tchaikovsky, the composer of *Swan Lake*, came up with his version well over a century ago.

Early indicators do not, however, look good: after an uncomfortable mimed television performance over the weekend, Victoria was booed at Birmingham's Party in the Park when her head set fell off half way through singing the new number – and her voice continued to be heard by the 30,000-strong crowd. "I couldn't believe she was miming," says one onlooker. But then again, as Victoria herself says, if it's all right for Britney Spears...

It is to be hoped that the aftermath of publicising Victoria's second single is less dramatic than last year's. In the middle of a promotional tour of Germany, while filming in a studio in Cologne, Victoria began to complain of a headache. The pain soon got worse, leading Victoria to suspect she had a migraine. Even that intensified, though, and so a doctor was summoned and said she should return home. Running a temperature of over 100°F, Victoria was forced to cancel her tour and was flown home in a private jet to Goff's Oak, where Jackie was on hand to look after her. There she was taken to the local medical centre and was diagnosed as having viral meningitis.

Everyone, Victoria included, was deeply shocked. Meningitis is one of those little known about but much feared diseases and the earliest reports even hinted that it could be fatal. When it emerged that it wasn't that type of meningitis, there was still widespread concern about Victoria's condition – and curiosity not least because, by one of those odd quirks of fate, Victoria is patron of the Meningitis Research Foundation.

While it wasn't life threatening, viral meningitis can be extremely serious, leading to sickness and headaches and sometimes resulting in a coma. Victoria saw a neurologist and had a lumbar puncture in order to rule out the more deadly form of the disease. Her type was not infectious, though, and is usually treated with rest and plenty of fluid. Often a sign that the patient is extremely run-down, viral meningitis can be caused by various different viruses, including the mumps virus, the herpes simplex virus and the virus which causes chicken pox and shingles.

If Victoria was infected through one of these viruses, it would indeed imply that her immune system was running on empty. In the vast majority of cases, however, viral meningitis is caused by a group called enteroviruses. A virus that caused gastroenteritis, for example, could spread to the lining (meninges) of the brain, which would cause viral meningitis.

"She doesn't look much like a pop star today, just my sick daughter," Jackie said. Tony was equally worried. "We were all shocked when we heard it was meningitis," he said. "She's very exhausted and we'll be looking after her until she gets better. Baby Brooklyn is fine." And Victoria's spokeswoman said, "She's had tests and she's been told to rest and not do anything. She's lying on the sofa at home with her mum looking after her." Beckham himself, of course, was beside himself with worry. In Paris to play for England against France, he rang Victoria up

to 10 times a day to check on her well-being and
that of Brooklyn but, reassured that his wife was
going to be OK, was able to stay on for the all
important game.

The timing couldn't have been worse. Apart
from her own single, Victoria was due to launch
the Spice Girls' next single *Holler* at the end of
September – it became the girls' ninth Number
One – which was followed by their third album
Forever, in November. It ended up at Number
Two in the UK charts and entered the US charts
at Number 39, which would have been deemed
a great success by most people but was, on Spice
terms, it was an abject failure.

At the beginning of September, however,
Victoria was in no fit state to do anything.
"Despite the tough schedule planned, she is
going to have to take it very easy," said a friend
at the time. "Victoria's doctors have ordered her
to rest for as long as it takes. It looks certain to
be a month or even longer before she can think
about working again. They have also told her
that her exhausting work schedule may even
have caused her strain of the bug. Victoria is

devastated that she has had to take time off. She is incredibly dedicated."

It was her first solid bout of time off since Brooklyn was born and Victoria was determined to fight back. She had to cancel an appearance to see her favourite designer, Maria Grachvogel, but in late September 2000, she managed to make it to the *Elle Magazine* Style Awards, where she spoke about her recent health scare. "I was terrified, I was afraid I was going to die," she said. "I'll never forget the moment they told me. It was shocking and it has really affected me. You always think the worst and you're afraid that it's all over."

Of course, apart from hiccups in her career (usually minor) little had really gone wrong for Victoria since she attended that fateful audition nearly six years previously. She was clearly finding it difficult to cope. "I've just been lying flat on my back," she said. "The doctors can't prescribe anything, so it's just a matter of waiting to get better. I still don't feel myself and it's testing my patience. I'm not drinking and it's difficult coming to things like this because I'm coughing and I still feel weak. It's frustrating not being able to do anything. I just have to slow down and pace myself." Even despite her weakened state, though, Victoria was in no mood to forgive and forget. "Where's that Spiller girl?" she asked. "I think she's avoiding me. I don't know why because I'm the one who made her famous. She must be scared after all the things she said about me." And so there you have it. Posh might have been beaten by Posher – and yet she was was still the one responsible for Sophie's success...

Shhhh!

12

The Colour of Money – Part II

She that is of the opinion money will do everything may well be suspected of doing everything for money. Benjamin Franklin

In just a few short years Victoria Beckham has become one of the richest female entertainers in Britain. The money making machine that was the Spice Girls has netted her millions, and if that were not enough, she has married one of the best paid footballers in the world – although her fortune is actually estimated to be even bigger than his. She was not going to go hungry (unless she wanted to) and neither was Brooklyn. The only question was: what would she do with all this money?

That turned out to be a very easy question to answer. Unlike her husband, Victoria already knew what it meant to be wealthy. Apart from the baron 18-month spell in Maidenhead as a young Spice Girl, she had never struggled –and £60 a week plus dole money was not exactly poverty. Her upbringing had been luxurious. She was used to fast cars and big houses, and now, for the first time, she could afford them on her own. It was time to start spending – and Victoria doesn't waste time.

First she hit the shops: then she got into property. In 1998, still a year before they got married, Victoria and David paid £300,000 for their penthouse flat in Alderley Edge in Cheshire. It provided them with a base in the north of England – close enough to Manchester to keep Sir Alex Ferguson happy – and one luxurious enough for Victoria. "It's an absolutely gorgeous flat," says one close friend.

"It's very modern, and they've spent a lot of money improving it, but it looks fantastic. I think David, especially, is very happy there. He has lots of his football pictures up on the walls. In a way, it feels more like his flat than hers." Despite Victoria's preference for the south of England, and her desire to be close to her family in Hertfordshire, the couple still use the flat, which is now thought to be worth more than £400,000.

Victoria and David are the archetypal modern couple and having moved in together, it was only a matter of time before they would do the decent thing and get engaged. As we saw earlier, David duly got down on one knee one night and produced a sparkling £40,000 ring, before popping the question. Then, in her now famous retort, Victoria cited Girl Power before declaring "What about me, will you marry me?" and upstaged her new fiancè with a £50,000 gold and diamond engagement ring of her own. Nouveau riche they may be, but you could never accuse the Beckhams of doing things on the cheap.

But for a Spice Girl and a footballer of David's standing, £300,000 for a flat and £90,000 for a couple of rings was not exactly breaking the bank. In fact, it was barely scratching the surface. The Beckhams are worth an estimated £30 million between them and while they are clearly ostentatious, their accountants are doing everything they can to minimise the tax the couple pay – and preserve their new-found riches.

Victoria and David have several accounts with Coutts, the Queen's bank. These include Victoria's business accounts – one in the name of "Moody Productions" and another under the name of "Yandella" (an anagram of "lean lady"). Although David shares private accounts at Coutts with Victoria, he also has a business account with Lloyds TSB, in the name of "David Beckham Limited."

Moody Productions was set up in 1997 and is the main channel for all of Victoria's earnings. Like the other Spice Girls, Victoria's business has always "hired" her to the band, or at least to "Spice Girls Limited", in exchange for a payment and a share of royalties. Other than that, her business doesn't actually do anything, but it almost certainly renders her liable for corporation tax as opposed to income tax, which is a clever way of minimising her tax bill. In the year to August 1998, she earned £6,066,364 – of which she received more than £1 million from OK!, a leading celebrity magazine – and a further £1 million from a publisher for writing a book.

In 1999, after the *de facto* break-up of the band had begun, she earned just £1,979,613 – almost £4 million less than the previous year – of which the majority, £1,500,000, came from the Spice Girls. Because Moody Productions is inactive, it makes little profit regardless of turnover, therefore, in all probability, further reducing her tax liabilities.

Of course where this money goes after leaving Moody Productions is not known, but the likelihood is that it goes into other companies, almost certainly offshore, to further minimise the tax Victoria has to pay the British Government. Moody Productions has just three directors, Victoria Caroline Beckham, Anthony William Adams and Jacqueline Doreen Adams. To put it another way, Posh, her mum and her dad.

Yandella is a smaller, newer, more complex company and also has just three directors, Victoria, Jacqueline and one David Robert Joseph Beckham. Officially, Posh and Becks own exactly half of the company each. The last accounts, for the year ending August 1999, show the company had assets (net current assets and total assets less current liabilities) of £80,832. But it's not quite that simple. The accounts also revealed that the company owed £596,280 (quite possibly to other companies with which they are involved), which means less corporation tax has to be paid as a result. It's perfectly legal and very tax efficient.

But the Beckhams' efficient tax management – to say nothing of their ostentatious lifestyle – doesn't impress everyone, with the result that they have even come to the attention of some politicians. Back in November 2000, one

Labour MP called for a "supertax" on the couple, using them as an example of Britain's many high-earners who "don't put enough in the public coffers."

Alan Simpson, MP for Nottingham South, attacked the "obscene" wealth of David and Victoria, and called for a new tax rate for all those earning more than £40,000 a week. He believes the public feel it is "grossly unfair" that those on middle incomes paid the same 40 per cent higher tax rate as multi-millionaires like Posh and Becks.

"When you start to talk to people about the superstar lifestyles, whether it's in the music industry or the salaries being paid weekly to the nation's footballers – the Beckhams of the world – the amount of money going to the super-rich is quite rightly viewed as obscene in itself," he says. "But it is grossly unfair when people who are on, say, £40,000 a year, are actually only in the same tax bracket with other people who are earning that amount per week.

"There is a broad consensus in society which says that the super-rich are getting off super-light in the tax regime. There is a realisation that those who are on lower and middle incomes predominantly pick up the tax contributions."

The truth is, Victoria and David don't really know how much tax they pay. Indeed, as one close friend of the couple reveals, Victoria and David don't even entirely understand how their own finances are managed, or concealed: "Other people have advised them how to obscure how much money they've got," he says. "Money is a driving force for them, yes, but only in terms of what it can buy. Money in itself doesn't mean anything to them. It's bought them freedom and it's bought them time. They leave it to other people – they don't understand it all and they don't really care about how it's done. But they definitely see that as a tap they wouldn't want turned off – so they've gone to their money people and said, 'We have this lifestyle that is more expensive than we can afford. How can we go on like this for as long as possible?'"

That attitude has also been echoed by Geri Halliwell, who said of her leaving the Spice Girls: "There seemed to be two traps I can fall into. One is definitely financial – having to struggle to fund an expensive lifestyle. The other is psychological – becoming addicted to fame. I don't want to suffer either fate."

Fame is, has been and always will be, a transient entity. It is a false messiah, a diversion from the moment, a tonic to the tough waters of celebrity. Geri, for all her faults, seems aware of this, but it is a lesson Victoria has yet to learn. Her spending goes on, unchecked, and her enthusiastic pursuit of celebrity, approval and financial reward is seemingly endless. It is a reality which David, because of his career, will have been warned about from an early age. Professional sportsmen are never allowed to suffer the illusion that their careers will last for the whole of their lives. They are expendable, and they know it. For pop stars, indulging them with illusions is all part of the business. They don't know they are going to fall from grace any moment – and the music industry wouldn't want them to.

Because of the very complex nature of their finances, it is impossible to be sure who owns what in the Beckham household, and how much both of them are worth individually. A reasonable estimate is that, to date, Victoria is worth £18 million, and her husband £12 million. But as David's earning power has increased in recent years, so Victoria's has diminished. And with the Spice Girls seemingly defunct, and her faltering solo career struggling to get off the ground, it could be that she has finally lost her role as the main breadwinner.

Until now though, she has always been the richer one – and she has shown it. She drives a Silver Mercedes CLK coupe, or, to put it another way, a £35,000 convertible. The £50,000 she spent on David's engagement ring was inevitable; just months earlier she had lavished an £11,000 diamond bracelet on him, too. To be fair to David, he did have the decency to respond in kind, by buying her a £13,000 Tiffany necklace.

Then, in July 2000, David spent £50,000 on a special anniversary present for Victoria. He secretly visited her favourite jeweller, Theo Fennel, and asked him to make a black diamond ring to match the £30,000 earrings he bought Victoria for her 26th birthday just two months earlier. And before that, for Christmas 1999, David paid £10,000 on a white baby grand piano for the couple – on the advice of Elton John. But even all this pales into insignificance when compared to Victoria's biggest gift to her husband: a Ferrari 550 Maranello that set her back an astonishing £220,000. Add to that the couple's seemingly endless private flights around the world each year, which cost £10,000 a time, and it is easy to see where the money goes.

But David is not the only recipient of Victoria's generosity. She also spent £10,000 on a facelift for her mother, £500,000 on houses for her brother and sister and £110,000 on a Porche Boxster and a top of the range Chrysler Jeep for her father. And just in case Brooklyn felt left out, she also shelled out a £1,000 on a mini Chrysler jeep for him .

Babies never come cheap, and Brooklyn certainly isn't an exception. As well as lavishing gifts and expensive designer clothing on their son, Victoria and David pay a small fortune every year to keep Brooklyn safely entertained. The couple do try to stay with him themselves as much as possible, but they still spend an estimated £20,000 a year on childcare. The fees at Brooklyn's nursery are by no means cheap, but even so, Victoria has paid for company for Brooklyn, by giving her sister Louise the money to enrol her two-year-old daughter Liberty at his nursery school. It would seem that, whatever the cost to his parents, Brooklyn Beckham will never be lonely. And there is no question that Victoria will do everything within her power to protect Brooklyn from the sort of unhappiness that at times plagued her during her formative years.

As for David's own finances, his company began 1999 with £111,616 in its account. That figure burgeoned to £326,194 at one stage, but then, of course, there was a rather expensive wedding in Ireland, which had to be paid for. At the end of the year, after bills had been fully deducted, that account had just £7,936 remaining in it – implying that the wedding had cost almost £320,000. Actually, it is estimated to have cost up to £500,000.

David may be one of the best footballers in the world, but even now, he is struggling to earn what his wife managed during the golden era of the Spice Girls. He earns £1,350,000 a year from his employers, Manchester United, although he is now re-negotiating his contract and according to sources within Old Trafford, he is set to become the club's best paid player on more than £50,000 a week, plus a further £1m a year loyalty bonus. This means, in wages from Manchester United alone, he will soon be earning close to £3,600,00 a year. Add to that future bonuses, signing on fees, promotional deals with the club and endorsements (last season he was given an extra £75,000 for winning the Premiership with Manchester United) and suddenly kicking a ball around looks like a very lucrative thing to do.

David Beckham is also lucky in that, not only is he a gifted footballer, but he has pop star looks to match. This naturally makes him a very attractive proposition for companies who want

him to endorse and promote their products –
and he knows it. He has a boot deal with Adidas
worth £1,400,000 and, back in 1999 he
negotiated a £1 million deal with Brylcreem and
a £500,000 deal with Sondico, the shin-pad
manufacturers. Even that, however, is small fry
compared to his most recent sponsorship tie-
ups: a £1million endorsement from Rage
Software to star as himself in a computer game
and a whopping £1,400,000 million from Police
Sunglasses to wear their products for the next
couple of years. Taken together, this means he
can expect to earn between £5 million and £6
million a year, at least in the immediate future.

Given their exorbitant spending habits, it's
just as well that both David and Victoria earn
millions of pounds each every year. To say David
has a soft spot for cars is rather like saying
Victoria is quite fond of designer clothes. He has
a Ferrari 360 Modena Berlinetta, which cost
£100,000, a Range Rover 4.6HSE worth
£70,000, a TVR Cerbera that set him back
£65,000 and a £40,000 Lincoln Navigator.
(That, of course, is in addition to his £220,00

Ferrari, but that doesn't really count as it was a gift from Victoria.)

Even after all this expenditure, however, the Beckhams were still building up to their major purchase. They were still living in a flat, albeit a penthouse, hundreds of miles from Victoria's family home in Hertfordshire. This meant the couple would very often spend nights apart, with Victoria opting to stay at her parents house in Goff's Oak – which was more convenient for London. Something simply had to be done. Cue a massive down payment on a massive investment, cue extravagance and cue luxury in all its meretricious tawdriness. Cue "Beckingham Palace".

Rowenbury House, as Beckingham Palace is more correctly, but less frequently called, is a mansion set in 24 acres of countryside at Sawbridgeworth in Hertfordshire. Victoria and David have already spent a fortune on renovating the property, which set them back £2.5 million when they bought it from the previous owners, Richard and Terri Maher, last year. The Maher's paid just £600,000 for the former council-run children's home when they bought it in 1997, but Posh and Becks obviously thought this level of opulence was well worth the cash.

And opulent it certainly is. Before you even get to the front door, you have to negotiate the gardens, on which the couple have spent more than £250,000. The flowerbeds are planted with more than 50,000 bulbs – and are scattered around a woodland paradise full of oak, maple, beech and sycamore trees. There is also plenty of manicured lawn and even a football pitch should David and Brooklyn fancy a quick kick about. There are also three themed gazebos – Lakeside, Ornamental and Romantic – a £70,000 barbeque and a tennis court. "The garden is very romantic. I want lots of bushes in the shape of hearts. I live in a complete fairy tale with things like that," says Victoria. Inside Rowenbury House though, is where the real money has been spent. There is a £100,000 recording studio (a gift to Victoria from David), a 100-ft swimming pool, a gym and a snooker room. At the top of an impressive oak staircase, there are a selection of en-suite bedrooms including their master suite.

"I've themed every room, it's really camp," says Victoria. "I've got an Audrey Hepburn bathroom, which is very romantic – wooden floors, black and white tiles, an old-fashioned bath and pictures everywhere of Audrey. I'm completely obsessed with her. There's a room like a tart's boudoir, with leopard print and mirrored ceiling. Then there's our bedroom, which is quite virginal and white, with a big four-poster, old oak bed.

"The hallway is completely camp, with bright red walls, a huge, great big, tacky chandelier and big thick, velvet curtains. There's a swimming pool area, the kitchen's baby blue and the lounge has a modern, hottish vibe, with big sofas, wooden floors and great big rugs. David's got a really cool snooker room for the boys – black and gold, with big plasma TVs – and I've got a gym, which I'll probably never actually go in."

But Victoria denies their lifestyle at Beckingham Palace is as luxurious as people believe. "People think I wander around the house in heels and a designer dress," she says. "But I have towelling dressing gowns and dodgy tracksuits. And Brooklyn isn't always the little angel everyone thinks. In fact, he's so-o-o-o naughty. He can make things really embarrassing for me sometimes. I've got white carpets and he has been sick all over them. He rides his scooter into my curtains too – so I'm used to sick and poo." And what about the name of the mansion? "I don't know if we'll actually re-name the house Beckingham Palace," says Victoria. "It's quite tongue-in-cheek and it makes me laugh, but there's a lot of cynical people that say, 'Who does she think she is?'" In truth, Victoria appears to be delighted with her new home's soubriquet.

One enormous priority for the Beckhams is security. Beckingham Palace has a half-mile long drive with a string of gates with entry-phones, which, combined with 24-hour security staff, CCTV cameras and burglar alarms, have helped them to forget several high-profile threats to their well-being. "Victoria and David want to feel safe wherever they are in the world, but especially at home," says one friend. "Unfortunately there are some very sick people about who seem to take a perverted pleasure in threatening them."

Noel Imber, a former lover of Louise Adams, Victoria's sister, was lucky enough to be given a guided tour of Beckingham Palace. He recalls being stunned by its sheer size, and the amount of money that must have spent on improving it. "About 10 people could stroll in through the front door, it's so big it's like a hotel," he says. "There's a huge staircase and bannisters and rooms coming off everywhere. And you can't miss an incredible chandelier, which took 10 people to put up.

"It has the largest dressing room I have ever seen. One side is dedicated to David and the other to Victoria. They have had cabinets built into the sides to display their jewellery and walk-in wardrobes. David's also got himself a bar and snooker room, which he has designed. He's got loads of football shirt all in frames on the walls. They are the ones he has swapped with some of the best players in the world and it looks awesome.

"To think that a man, woman and child will be the only ones living in it is unbelievable. Victoria told me it had cost two and a half million and Louise told me they had spent the same again doing it up. It has a swimming pool, sunbeds and every mod con you could think off.

"It will be their permanent base. Victoria and David feel it is somewhere where they should be together – their inner sanctum. It will be their special place where they feel safe and homely. David and Victoria try to live a normal life but obviously with the designer clothes, the mansion and their fantastic cars it's not normal. They can have virtually anything they want."

The roof of Brooklyn's £20,000 nursery, which depicts the night sky, came in a flash of inspiration to David when he was shopping at the Trafford Centre in Manchester, which has an identical theme. The stars in Brooklyn's room are said to be so life-like they even change like the real sky between dusk and dawn. One friend who has seen the nursery says: "It looks fantastic. Most kids have a mobile above their heads but Brooklyn's got the whole sky to look at." Interior designers worked on the nursery, which also has Disney cartoon characters dotted around the walls. The couple wanted the fairytale room to be sumptuously luxurious for the two-year-old, and it took them several months to finalise the details. A spokesman for the Trafford Centre, which proved the inspiration for David, says: "The complete constellation changes in a typical night. That's why it cost so much to install. We are delighted David and Victoria were so impressed by it. They are always here shopping and will have seen just how fabulous our roof looks."

The amazing "night sky" effects on Brooklyn's ceiling are created by projectors built into his bedroom walls. They change the colour and layout of the sky as he sleeps. The nursery took six months to build, but then: "Money was no object," according to the friend.

But unlike the flashy engagement rings, designer clothes and fast cars, the £5 million the couple have spent on Beckingham Palace is not to be taken lightly. When you're as rich as the Beckhams, £70,000 for a car, or £10,000 for a facelift is easily afforded. But to spend nearly a fifth of your fortune on a "fairytale palace" is not, to put it mildly, cautious. The couple will have to continue earning millions for some years to come entirely to justify the sums spent so far.

David and Victoria's flamboyant spending may be a cause for national amusement, but it is less likely to entertain their accountants. While In terms of tax management the couple have clearly been well advised, they have been less sensible with the rest of their finances – particularly for two people in such fickle careers. At the moment, David is at the peak of his footballing career and Victoria continues to make a good living from her music and Spice Girls' royalties – but neither will last forever. In fact, this extraordinarily famous and wealthy couple are in many ways as vulnerable as the rest of us – and in some ways more so.

The reality for the Beckhams is this: they are perched precariously on the precipice of obscurity. For the moment they are fascinating couple, both of whom spend a fortune on each other and expensive trinkets, but it's not a lifestyle that is easy to maintain. They are royalty for the 21st century, the king and queen of a celebrity circus – a circus that always, eventually, moves on. The harsh reality for David and Victoria is that they could be humbled in a matter of months. One bad tackle for David, a couple of disastrous albums for Victoria and the public will lose interest – they always do.

To his credit, David seems to be taking precautions against the inevitable end of his footballing career. He recently signed up to a specially tailored "Footballer's Financial Plan" with the couple's bank, Coutts, in order to safeguard against enforced retirement from the game. The package includes investment advice, special disability insurance and mortgages suited to players relatively short playing careers.

"Players like David are earning more than ever and while they still spend money on celebrity trappings, like sports cars, country mansions and parties, they must also realise they now have to put a portion of their money into investments," says one City insider. "They have to learn from the mistakes of other soccer stars over the years. If David and Victoria aren't careful, regardless of what their incomes now may be, their money will soon be eaten up by their lavish lifestyle."

If Victoria needs convincing that vast amounts of money could soon evaporate, she need look no further than one of her fellow Spice Girls, Mel B, who has already learned the lessons of financial management the hard way. Mel B met the man she was to marry, Jimmy Gulzar, in 1998 when he was hired as a dancer for the Spice Girls' world tour. Within three months of their first meeting, she was pregnant and the couple were married within a year. But money soon became a destructive force in their relationship, and when Gulzar, who himself had come from a poverty-stricken immigrant family in Amsterdam, became addicted to the high life, events took a turn for the worse. Indeed his shopping sprees became almost legendary soon earning him the nickname "Jimmy Goldcard".

* * *

The couple tried everything to resolve their problems, including joint marriage guidance counselling sessions and, in a desperate bid to stop his exorbitant spending, Gulzar also visited a psychotherapist. But money had driven a wedge between the couple and, after a series of furious rows, they split up on January 1, 2001. Mel B immediately left her mansion in Little Marlow, Buckinghamshire, and flew to America with their 18-month-old daughter Phoenix Chi. Trouble lay ahead.

Gulzar, who has just recently launched his own singing career, had become accustomed to the celebrity lifestyle – and he wasn't going to let go of it without a fight. He demanded a £10 million settlement, almost half of Mel B's estimated £22 million fortune. Unfortunately for him, his ex-wife wasn't too keen on giving up half her wealth – and offered him £750,000 in cash and a £500,000 flat in London instead. They argued, both in and out of the media spotlight, and Mel B hired a big-hitting lawyer to "do everything in his power" to ensure she kept her money.

341

"I am a very traditional person," she said at the time. "And if you get pregnant, you get married, and you make it work, and I was madly, 100 per cent in love with Jim. That's why we had a baby and got married and I have no regrets. It's been draining, but I know I gave my everything to make it work. It was just unfortunate that I had a relationship where I let a man crush my spirit. He tried to change the things about me that had made him fall in love with me. A lot of men do that. I felt very vulnerable and insecure about myself and I let that happen. I don't blame anyone for that, only myself.

"But you can only be depressed for so long before you start to bore yourself. He's the father of my child and a very good dad, so I will help him out financially because Phoenix will be staying with him a lot and I want her to be in a nice, clean, safe environment. But beyond that, I think that's where my responsibilities stop."

Ultimately of course, the courts ruled that Gulzar was not entitled to half her fortune after just two years of marriage. Instead Mel agreed to pay him £700,000 – a £620,000 lump sum and a further £100 a week until their two-year-old daughter Phoenix Chi is 18 – an outcome, although less than her original offer, that Gulzar declared he was "well satisfied" with.

The point, however, had been made. Money can disappear very easily indeed, even if you're a Spice Girl – and particularly when you have a demanding ex-husband and an expensive lifestyle. And although Victoria and David are independently wealthy and seem very happy together, they are perhaps the least frugal couple in Britain. Add to that the fact that they are close friends with Sir Elton John, who famously managed to blow £40 million in a spending spree which lasted less than two years, and it is easy to see why now is the time for sensible investment, not reckless spending. After all, when the time does come, David and Victoria will both have a very long retirement and, even with their combined finances, if they "did an Elton", they would pay a very severe financial penalty.

For Victoria, wealth and all its glorious trappings have been a welcome by-product of the fame she has always wanted. She came from a wealthy background and it was the public acclaim and the media attention she craved, not the money. Victoria Beckham has always been wealthy, and there is no doubt she would be lost without her new riches, but it is fame that drives her. But just as with her celebrity, she is slowly beginning to realise a harsh but inescapable truth about money. Getting it is one thing. Holding onto it is another.

Shhhhh! **13**

All in the Family

I don't trust anyone but my family implicitly.
Victoria Beckham

The two most important people in Victoria's life are her husband David and her son Brooklyn. There then follow, in no particular order, her parents, Tony and Jackie, and her brother and sister, Christian and Louise. They are the inner circle, the only people Victoria really trusts, and no one else can get anywhere near them. They are Victoria's refuge when she's tired of being Posh Spice, they comfort her when she's down and they look after her when she's ill. Before Victoria and David were able to move – Beckingham Palace, Victoria divided her time between the Alderley Edge penthouse and Goff's Oak, where it is significant that she still sleeps in the bedroom she inhabited as a child. Victoria doesn't do friendship in the way many people do: for her the priorities are family and career. And that's it.

This closeness within the family and between the siblings was fostered in childhood by the protective Tony and Jackie, who liked to keep an eye on their children at all times. "I remember when we were younger we weren't allowed to go out on our bikes and things," says Louise. "And we weren't allowed to play in the street with other kids. But looking back I can see why they were so concerned – we were in the middle of nowhere. But we'd play in the garden, we had a big swimming pool, we'd have friends round. We could do anything we wanted, as long as we didn't leave the house or the garden."

So in some respects it was like a prison – but a gilded one. Perhaps, Victoria inhabits a similar prison in her current life. As a child, she couldn't go anywhere she wanted on a whim and as an adult, she can't either. The difference is that while it was formerly her parents who clipped her wings, it is now the weight of her celebrity. If she goes out, she gets noticed. Victoria, one way or another, has always been under scrutiny.

Christian was the only boy, and the youngest child, at that. Like many younger brothers, he both loved and was embarrassed by, his sisters. "It was nice in a way with two sisters, but I often wished I had a brother as well, which, with David, I feel that I have now," he says. "With the girls, there'd be lots of make-up and stuff around, which I've sort of got used to now, and the bathrooms would be messy. But they used to embarrass me more than anything. They'd get dressed in my room because it had a long mirror where they could dry their hair and there'd be glitter all over my clothes."

The family has certainly always been versed in the work ethic, which again stood Victoria in good stead when she joined the Spice Girls. It came from Tony, who, when the trio were children, was building up his business. "When we were younger, he had offices," says Louise, "and he used to leave before we got up and then by the time he got home at night, we'd be in bed. I think it taught us that if you want something, you've really got to work for it."

Victoria is not the only performer in the family. Both siblings have also dabbled in show business, as indeed did Tony in his band The Sonics three decades earlier. Christian's involvement was minimal, he did some modelling when he was young, but grew tired of it. Louise, though, went a lot further. She actually started out along the same route as Victoria when she was a child, and even appeared in commercials and the children's programme *Dramarama*, but simply didn't have the dedication required to continue. "I was a real show-off," she says. "My mum says I still am. Victoria and I used to go dancing together and we both had agents. I used to do quite a bit of television and modelling work when I was younger – I used to work more than her, actually – but then I just got bored of going to castings."

And Louise, unlike Victoria, went through a rebellious streak as a teenager. "I think I was horrible to my mum and dad, when I think of it now," she says. "And I used to fight with Victoria because she wasn't the sort of person who wanted to go out all the time and hang about with people she knew she shouldn't. But I couldn't understand why I couldn't hang around in the streets until 12 o'clock at night when I was 14. But Victoria never wanted to. Then she left home at 16 to go to dancing college. I remember her saying that one day she went away leaving behind a little brother and when she came back her brother was a man! She went away when I was a young girl and she came back when I was pregnant!"

When she came back, Victoria was also a member of the Spice Girls. "I just remember them being really loud," Louise says. "Mel B got her boobs out for Christian! Well, she had a bra on and she just sort of flashed her bra at him. He was only young." Christian also remembers the girls in the early days. "I used to come home with my friends from school," he says, "and they'd all be there and I used to go to my room or just go out," he says. "They were really loud."

Other than the loudness, Louise and Christian were thrilled as their sister's rise to fame began and they still are. There is still petty sibling rivalry between the sisters, usually involving who wears what first, but it is entirely superficial. Louise is very much the little sister, looking up to Victoria and occasionally accompanying her to events when David is not available, but it is clear that Victoria relies on her a great deal.

And amazingly, members of Victoria's family, especially Louise, have shown no jealousy or resentment about the fact that one of their number has gone global. Quite the opposite, in fact. Victoria's parents positively swell with pride when confronted with the achievements of their eldest, as witnessed by Tony's speech at the wedding, in which he emphasised his daughter and son-in-law's success, while her brother and sister have been only too happy to share in the advantages that celebrity has brought in its wake. Especially Louise.

Louise Adams is a pretty girl, with a strong resemblance to her older and more famous sister. She has the same facial features as Victoria and the same slim build, although she is slightly shorter than Victoria's height of 5'6. She is also Victoria's friend, companion and confidante. She protects her fiercely and she is one of the few people allowed to criticise her. "When we're out and Victoria goes to the toilet, I have to go with her," she says. "I'm like her bodyguard. When a girl says something nasty, I scream back."

Nor is this protective streak confined to going out together. If people write something about Victoria that upsets her, it upsets the family, too. "It's very upsetting when people say Victoria's anorexic," says Louise. "Her picture once appeared in a newspaper next to a piece by a journalist who said she looked 'skeletal and disgusting.' Next to it was a picture of the journalist, who was minging. I phoned the journalist to have a go, but you couldn't print what I said. I'm always telling her that her skirts are too short, though." "They are sisters, but more importantly, they are cracking good friends," says an observer. "They are such close mates. If one hurts, the other cries."

And if one is successful, the other benefits. If Victoria bears comparison to Princess Diana and Madonna, then Louise, alas, may be seen as another Meg Matthews, the erstwhile wife of Noel Gallagher, who also became well known by association. It must be said, however, that Louise does not give the impression of being as profligate as Meg; neither does she share Meg's rather dubious taste in clothes. It is well known that Meg is also a devotee of intoxicants, but this is far from being the case with Louise. Her addictions – like her sister's – would appear to be clothes and publicity.

Like Meg, however, Louise raises hackles for enjoying a kind of fame that she has not actually earned herself. She accompanies Victoria all over the world, she dresses like her, she dates footballers like her and she seems to enjoy the trappings of celebrity quite as much as her sister does. In the joint worlds of pop and fashion, bitchiness is never far away and there have been a good many mutterings that Louise has only got to where she is because she has a world-famous sister. Louise refutes this charge. "People have said to me before, 'Oh, you think you're this, you think you're that,'" she says. "But you don't change, people around you change. You have a lot of people trying to be your friend."

Christian, on the other hand, has largely stayed out of the limelight and holds down an ordinary job. Neither does Victoria employ him (she has used Louise as a personal assistant). "I stayed on [at school] for a year in the sixth form, then left and didn't really know what I wanted to do," he says. "But I got a job in computers – and I'm still there. I build, repair and install computers for a company in Cheshunt. I used to do some work for my dad, but it didn't really appeal to me."

Like Victoria, Louise did not excel academically, but unlike her sister, she was not prepared to put in the slog required to become famous, and were it not for Victoria she would

almost certainly still be in a more mundane job.
After she left school, Louise went to secretarial
college, but decided it didn't suit her. She also
trained as a hairdresser – as did her mother and
both of David's sisters – and manicurist, she
worked as a buyer for a mobile phone company
and she temped in London for a quantity
surveyor and an accountant. While Victoria was
achieving world fame with the Spice Girls,
Louise was working as an administrative
assistant in a high street bank.

She doesn't any more. All this changed when
Victoria became a star. None of what she had
done previously was an obvious preparation for
what she has done in the years since her sister
became a Spice Girl: Louise has become a
boutique owner, a Sky TV presenter – for which
she was paid a reported £55,000 – a columnist
in *Looks* magazine and an "Ultimate Party Girl"
for Vladivar Vodka, following in the footsteps of
Sara Cox – and, naturally, Meg Matthews.
Louise, however, does not like the suggestion
that this came about because of Victoria's fame.
"I've been offered a lot of jobs in the business,

but I'm taking my time sorting through them," she says. "It's hard because whatever I do I'll get criticised. But I'll have to deal with it – I know I can handle it." To be honest, it's unlikely Louise would be criticised had she chosen to work as a secretary rather than presenting *Smash Hits* on Sky, but no matter. What's the point of having a famous sister if you, too, can't have a bit of fun?

And, like Victoria, Louise has become adept at changing her appearance, most recently when she got a complete makeover for the Vladivar shot. Her nose was heavily shaded to shave off some width, her skin was given an all over golden glow by lashings of St Tropez tan – Victoria's favourite – her eyebrows were reshaped and she was given a fringe and high ponytail, created with a hairpiece. She is, in fact, becoming more glamorous by the day and in that she has something in common with Victoria, too. Neither are natural beauties but both have created an image for themselves through sheer determination.

Victoria has also employed her as a personal assistant, which gave Louise the opportunity to increase her own wardrobe. "I share a lot of clothes with Victoria," she says. "We are both the same size. It is really lucky for me because she gets sent loads of designer freebies. She is really generous. When a load comes in she'll say, 'Pick out what you like.'"

Louise doesn't exactly help to put a stop to the comparisons between herself and Victoria. When she accompanied Victoria, still recovering from a bout of viral meningitis, to the *Elle* style awards in September 2000, the pair were sporting matching hair extensions. Like Victoria, she has also had breast enhancement surgery and showed off her new figure at the 1999 Brits Awards, wearing a tiny satin corset. "Louise couldn't wait to show her new breasts off," says a friend. "She paid enough money for her new look and was desperate to have the surgery in time for the Brits. She loves the limelight as much as Victoria. There was no way she was going to pass up an opportunity like this."

And unlike Victoria, Louise is very open about the work she has had done. "I tried to keep it quiet, but I hadn't even gone for the anaesthetic and I got a call from my mum saying, 'The press know,'" she says. "So I don't know, someone had obviously seen me go in. I booked in under another name and everything and I only told my two close friends. But there's no use worrying about it because it's pretty obvious I've had it done. I'm very pleased with it. I didn't have boobs and I wanted them."

It can be amusing to hear the way Louise talks about her new silhouette. "I can wear things and feel more confident," she says. "When you've had it done, everyone wants to see them, people are like, 'Ooh, can I have a look?' But you don't mind much because you don't feel like their yours, it's like wearing something and showing people."

Louise's ex-boyfriend, Noel Imber, tells how this provoked some sibling rivalry between the two. "Victoria had a very subtle breast lift in 1999," he says. "It cost £10,000 and she went up to a B-cup. But then Louise had her boobs done – an operation paid for by their mother – and Victoria decided hers still weren't big enough so earlier this year she had another op. She came round to Louise's house after having them done. I was there. She complained how much they hurt her. But she was very happy with the way they looked and told Louise that David loved them."

Like Victoria, Louise seems to be developing a taste for plastic surgery. In July 2001, it emerged that she was spending £3,000 on laser treatment around the eyes to get rid of wrinkles. She shrugged off suggestions that 24 was rather young to have the treatment and said of the rash and bruising it caused around her eyes, "I know I look terrible but you're meant to start this laser course while you're young. I'll have the lot when I'm older."

The two even shop at the same boutiques and used to buy many items of clothing from a little place called Tarts, located on Waltham Cross High street, very close to Beckingham Palace. "The shop's not too classy, which is why you see carloads of girls pulling up outside and charging in because we don't intimidate them," says the shop's owner, Brenda Gawen. "Victoria has been here in her PJs. It was about 6pm and she just popped down to look for something to wear that night."

One of Brenda's specialities is basques, which she gets made up from a dressmaker in Leeds, who was on the verge of going broke before Brenda discovered him. "He'd spent his last tenner on a sewing machine," she recalls. "And I heard he could run up a good basque to order for a fraction of the cost designers charge. Victoria loves them and she's bought a few – though you don't see her wearing them in the papers. I think they're for her and David in private. She has a white one, a lilac one and a pink one. I think David asks her to wear things at home sometimes so they can save certain things for themselves."

Victoria's tastes are not always exclusively with the top designers, according to Brenda. "She's sent the Gucci stuff, but she always says it's too big," she says. "Designer gear doesn't tend to fit all our trendy little customers. A lot of designers send her cases full of samples and she picks out which pieces she likes. But it's not like going out shopping for yourself. I think that's why she comes – Tarts – so she can choose for herself."

And, of course, Louise was also a regular customer. "In fact, she's in here every other day," said Brenda. "She likes to get the clothes first because I think there's a bit of rivalry going on. Victoria has often mentioned she's after something similar to an outfit we'd previously sold to Louise. And if I give an outfit to Louise to pass on to Victoria, I don't always know if it will get to her because they're the same size – an eight on the bottom half and a ten on top."

The girls fell out with Brenda, though, after Victoria accused her of using her famous client's name to garner more publicity, and Louise has now opened her own boutique, a shop called The Closet in Cuffley, Hertfordshire. It is just 12ft by 6ft and fits snugly in between a fishing tackle shop and a mobile phone store. Prices range from £30 to £300 and Louise sells bustiers, T-shirts, denim skirts and suits by Kyri, Jimmie B and Leaf Designs, as well as clothes she designed herself. All of that time put in shopping with Victoria has clearly been put to good use and although it's early days, the shop appears to be doing well.

Of course, as she is so close to Victoria, Louise sees the downside of celebrity at close hand. And while she realises that had Victoria not made it, then she, Victoria would not have met David Beckham, made lots of money and become a big star, Louise sometimes wishes the two could go back to the way they were before the Spice Girls came along. "I just think, wouldn't it be nice if people could leave Victoria alone for two minutes?" she says. "There's things you can't do. Like Christian and I will say, 'Oh, we're just popping to the shops.' And Victoria says, 'I'd really like to come,' but when she comes, people won't leave you alone. It would be nice if she could come out with us and be normal. She is normal, it's just that people treat her differently."

Victoria has managed to do most things first. She became successful, got married and is quite clearly the leader in the sisterly relationship. Louise did, however, manage to come first in the mother stakes. "It was a real big shock to me! [finding out she was pregnant]," she says. "I didn't know I was pregnant for two months. I thought my dad was going to be angry but he wasn't. He just cuddled me and I cried. I hadn't cried about it before but I think it was just a relief, a feeling of, 'Well everyone knows, now; I can just get on with it." Christian was more pragmatic. When the news came out that Victoria was also pregnant, he grumbled about having not one but *two* single mothers in the family. Victoria, of course, spared his blushes by getting married to Brooklyn's father four months after the baby's birth.

Louise's daughter Liberty was born on May 24 1998, prompting an outpouring of broody musings from her sister. "When I saw Liberty, I couldn't believe how tiny and beautiful she was," says Victoria. "It was amazing to hold her in my arms. Usually when I hold babies I feel worried but not with my own niece. I felt far more comfortable. I even changed her nappy."

Louise sadly broke up with Liberty's father Stephen Lawrence, an air-conditioning engineer, when Liberty was just four months old and it is only recently that she has looked as if she will soon be settling down again. However, Liberty sees her father regularly and the two have stayed in touch. "He sees her now and he's a very good dad," she says. "He has her most weekends, which is nice because it gives me a chance to do what I want to do and gives him a chance to spend time with her."

Not that Louise wanted to settle down until now. She has become a fixture on the celebrity circuit, with or without Victoria, and she has shown little sign of wishing to change the new status quo. But she doesn't like to admit it – too much. "I wouldn't call myself the ultimate party girl because I'm not out that much," she says. "People say I'd go to the opening of a fridge, but it's not true. It's just that whenever I go out, I get my picture taken, so it looks like I go everywhere."

Actually, despite remaining close to the parental home in Goff's Oak, it is clear that Louise thoroughly enjoys a night out on the tiles. "I get invited to loads of places and parties, and I know a lot of girls would love to be in that position," she says. "I never queue to get – a club. I'll go to a place in London and there'll be massive queues and the blokes on the door will be like, 'Come in Louise,' and I'll walk past with 15 friends. And then I do think, 'Is that a nice thing to do?' But when it's raining and there's a queue of about 30 minutes to get in, what woman in her right mind wouldn't do it? I do think about it, though, and sometimes it strikes me that I'm being quite rude not to remember how lucky I am."

The similarities between the sisters extend to men. Like Victoria, Louise has a penchant for footballers, dating Ryan Giggs – Victoria had a poster of him up in her room in the early Spice years – and Noel Imber who, like David, had shorn hair, pierced ears and a liking for smart sunglasses. In fact, he was even mistaken for the England captain on occasion. He was 24 at the time of their relationship and was a goalkeeper for non-league Hertfordshire club Boreham Wood earning £130 a week. He was also a part-time gardener, which led to some rather churlish remarks about the dissimilarities between him and Louise's famous brother in law. "He might look like Becks but he's not in the same financial league," said a team-mate sniffily. "In fact, he's been known to have to cadge a few quid off some of the lads." She has also dated Dave Gardner, a Manchester United apprentice.

The relationship didn't last long and before meeting Haydn Isted earlier this year, of which more below, Louise said, "The truth is, I'm not in a serious relationship at all. At the moment, I am just going out with my friends and enjoying myself. Marriage and relationships aren't something I think about a lot. Having Liberty, I have to be careful what men I introduce her to."

Noel gives a revealing insight into Victoria and David's life together, a life Louise is hoping to emulate with Haydn. "They are the most perfectly compatible couple I have ever met," he says. "They can't keep their hands off each other and you could feel this tremendous spark between them. He doesn't need anyone but her. If they've been apart – even for a few hours – when they get home it's like a special occasion."

He also tells of a special dinner David made for Victoria when he had to miss Valentine's Day. "He lit candles and placed them all around the dining room table – it looked fantastic," he says. "But they just sat down in their trainers and tracksuits and seemed totally absorbed in each other. Posh is always going on about 'my gorgeous David.' When they are apart, they are constantly on the phone or sending text messages. They are so close that it sometimes seems they are joined at the hip."

Louise gets on well with David – in fact, had David not initially got on with the whole Adams family, it is highly unlikely the relationship could have progressed. "I find it easier talking to David, sometimes, than talking to my sister," she says. "I know that he accepts me as a sister because he takes the mickey out of me and winds me up all the time. He phones me up and he puts voices on and says he'd like to offer me a job modelling. Then he says that it's modelling balaclavas. I'm like, thanks David." Like Victoria, David is generous to Louise. "He once bought Victoria loads of underwear," she says, "and he must have felt sorry for me so he got me some, too. They were very unsexy. Big shorts and a vest. But the thought was there."

Christian is also extremely fond of his brother-in-law and remembers the first time they met. "It was when he first came to our home," he says. "He arrived in the middle of the night and my mum and dad came down to meet him in their dressing gowns! I thought he was really nice. Really quiet."

It is hardly surprising that Louise is constantly compared to Victoria, but she genuinely doesn't seem to understand why. "It makes me laugh when I hear that," she says. "But what can I do. We're sisters, we look like each other. Lots of sisters do, it's just not something I can help. And as for copying Victoria, that's just rubbish. We go shopping together and often pick the same things. But what really annoys me is when I buy something and then she borrows it and gets her photograph splashed all over the front pages of the newspaper. And then I think, 'Bloody hell. I can't wear that now, can I.' But we're sisters, and it's just us."

Louis shares a house in Goff's Oak with Christian, bought for them by Victoria (she previously lived in a smaller house nearby, also purchased by her generous sister.) It has four bedrooms, two bathrooms and is so close to the Adams' house that the garden of the latter can be seen from the top floor. There is even talk of creating a path between the two properties.

The house is full of pictures of the family: Victoria with Liberty in the dining room, all the siblings together for Louise's birthday at the Sugar Reef restaurant in London to say nothing of the wedding pictures of David and Victoria. In her bedroom, Louise has a large, wrought iron four-poster while the rest of the house is a combination of light, Shaker-style wood on staircases, doors and kitchen furnishings and darker, ethnic style carved furniture and *objets d'art*. There is a carved elephant that guards the staircase, a sculpted giraffe's head on the stairwell and a modern take on an art deco fireplace in the sitting room.

And although she loves spending time in London, remaining in the area where she grew up suits Louise. She can go about unnoticed, as can Victoria. "Round here, people still don't even take much notice of Victoria, do they?" she says. "They notice David, but I think that's because he's not around here very much."

Victoria is paying for Liberty to attend the same nursery school as Liberty's higher profile cousin Brooklyn so that the two will grow up to be friends as well as cousins. And Louise has also suffered the downside of celebrity, even if it is by association – she has had a stalker. In November 2000, she was forced to call the police after the tyres of her A-Class Mercedes were slashed outside her house for the second time. "I'm worried about my safety," she said at the time. "I drive along looking in my mirror wondering if anyone is following me."

This year, however, Louise's luck changed, at least so far as her love life was concerned. In March 2000, she met Haydn Isted, a 27-year-old businessman from Isleworth, Middlesex. The two hit it off immediately, and Louise was soon introduced to Haydn's parents – a meeting about which she felt nervous. "I'm shy if I have to meet new people, like when I had to meet my boyfriends' parents for the first time," she says. "You don't want to do or say anything wrong."

Haydn, however, was clearly smitten. "Louise is really lovely and all my mates think so," he says. "She's really down to earth and makes an effort to get on with everybody." And just three months after they met, Haydn proposed during a short break in Dublin. After Louise accepted, he presented her with a £10,000 ring.

The wedding is expected to take place in 2002, and although it is extremely unlikely to be on the scale of David and Victoria's, Louise's tastes are not as simple as she would sometimes have us believe. "I'd love for us to be able to go abroad and get married, but my mum would kill me," she says. "She'd hit the roof." Haydn also says, "We don't want a traditional wedding," but chances are it will make something of a splash…

Shh**hh**! **14**

Queen of
Herts

A nd so to Victoria's multi-million pound
question: what next? At the time of
writing, she has a new single and a new album
coming out, and an enormous amount depends
on their performance. If they are successful she
will have bought herself more time as a pop
star – if not, well, it may be time to start all
over again. Victoria has been promoting the
single as only she knows how, touring up and
down the country, giving interviews to all,
sundry and Jerry Springer and even adopting a
new look.

Gone, for the moment at least is the Gucci sophisticate and in its place is a rock chick. Victoria has been appearing in leathers, jeans and a bandanna, and has even been seen sporting a lip ring – which immediately prompted criticism from parents concerned that their children will likewise opt for the pierced-lip look. Like her live singing which turned out to be mimed, though, it turned out that appearances were deceptive – the ring was not real.

But Victoria is at a cross roads and she knows it. She's got the money, she's got the man, but she works in one of the most precarious businesses in the world and it could all fade away tomorrow. In the past, she's been quite level headed about this. "Fame can be taken away from you as easily as it can be given to you," she said, "and a lot of celebrities forget that. Everybody can love you one moment, but everybody can turn against you the next."

True enough, and Victoria has already experienced some of the down side of the celebrity lifestyle. But observers of Sophisticated Spice have noticed a change in her character in recent years, a change that could bring about a whole new set of problems of its own. Namely, she's beginning to believe her own publicity. She's beginning to think that she truly deserves the good fortune that has come her way, and has forgotten that luck and hard work have played a large part.

And this change seemed to start to appear when she married David Beckham and thus became half of the most famous couple in Britain. She has outshone the rest of the Spice Girls, she is now, if anything, more famous for being half of Posh and Becks than she was as Posh Spice and she's beginning to act in a way that reflects her own true importance, as she sees it, rather than as a nice girl who's made good. "She's changed beyond all recognition in the past four years, from being a nice, local Hertfordshire girl to someone with a vastly inflated idea of her own importance," says Nick Stern, a photographer who has followed her career closely. "She thinks she's royalty."

That may well be true. Quite apart from the tiara she wore for her wedding and the thrones the couple sat on – appropriate for the coronation of Posh and Becks – Victoria does not discourage people from calling her home Beckingham Palace. In fact, she has developed a new website, www.victoriabeckham.mu, which is either a tongue in cheek look at her own celebrity or a pop star bidding a final farewell to any last grasp of reality, depending on your point of view.

The website, which is a cartoon version of the lives of David and Victoria, is so kitsch as to be almost ironic. The viewer is led up a long drive to the front door, which an animated version of Victoria opens wearing what would appear to be a Gucci two piece. "Welcome to Beckingham Palace," she says in an accent that is far more high street than *haute couture*, before leading the viewer inside. Here we find three thrones – one for David, one for Victoria and one for baby Brooklyn.

Viewers can play music on the stereo, play computer games in Brooklyn's room and find as much information about the iconic couple as they like. It's not clear whether Victoria is aware of the impact of the cartoon house on the unexpecting viewer, but one commentator compared it to Elvis's Graceland home: not least because it has a Royal Bathroom, featuring side by side lavatories with D and V written on the cisterns over them. The real house does not have such a room, although Victoria confessed they thought about it.

Victoria says she is not taking this seriously. "It's quite tongue-in-cheek," she says. "I'm only having a joke. It makes me laugh that people don't get that." That's as maybe, but in the world of pop celebrity it can be easy to confuse fact and fantasy. On this one, the jury is still out...

Nor is Victoria's website the only cartoon that will be featuring the couple in the near future. Giles Pilbrow, the man behind *Have I Got News For You* and *Spitting Image* has a new show that will be coming out in autumn 2001: 2DTV. It will feature cartoon versions of a whole range of celebrities, politicians and royalty, including Prince William, Geri Halliwell, Tony Blair, Catherine Zeta Jones, Michael Douglas and, of course, David and Victoria. It is not a flattering take on the couple: a stick thin Victoria is seen constantly bullying her husband and pushing him around. "They're constantly getting lost in their palatial home and she is constantly bullying him," said a spokesperson for ITV. "It's very good and it's got a very big future."

And next, of course, is the issue of more children. Both Beckhams want to increase their brood, with perhaps four children in total. But the timing has to be right and for now, at least, career comes first. "Victoria is a very determined person," says Noel Imber, Louise's ex. "Neither she nor David want their son Brooklyn to be an only child, but she insists the album must come first. Louise told me they are planning to have lots more kids – maybe two or three more – and they don't care if they are boys or girls.

"Brooklyn is a great little lad and he gets on with his cousin Liberty really well. They spend a

lot of time together and you can tell he'd love a
brother or sister. But Victoria wants to get the
album out of the way and then start trying
again. David will be thrilled when they do. But
Victoria is hard-headed and insists on the final
say. David is even more excited than her at the
prospect of new kiddies. He has been the
perfect, doting dad from day one – changing the
nappies, bringing up his wind. He says he
recommends fatherhood to anyone.

"Victoria has got it all mapped out and
knows the direction she wants her life to go.
She's written a wonderful song about Brooklyn
for her new album and is really excited about it.
But once the record is out – and hopefully doing
well – she can relax enough to try to get
pregnant again." In many ways, this is actually
quite sensible. If Victoria doesn't make it as a
solo artist now, she might not have the chance
to have another go, whereas she is still young
enough to put off having more children for a
time. Nor will she have forgotten that Virgin
Records were not best pleased when she and
Mel B became pregnant – and with an up-and-

coming album and single, it is no time to antagonise your record label.

The Spice Girls themselves would appear to be over. Mel C, who has suffered from depression in the last few years, let the cat out of the bag when she said that she was no longer a part of the band. "I will always be a Spice Girl but I don't intend to do any more work with the Spice Girls," she said in March. Frantic denials were issued. "There's no way we are splitting up," said Victoria in an interview the next day. "I don't know exactly what Mel said, but I talk to the other two girls all the time. All three of us want to keep going with the band, I'm completely certain of that. We're definitely going to carry on. I would be the first to know if we're breaking up and we're not."

Brave words, but it is very hard indeed to see how the girls could carry on without Mel C, long acknowledged to be the real talent in the band. And it is not surprising that it is Victoria who issued such an urgent denial: given that she herself has acknowledged her voice is not all it could be, she would clearly rather carry on as part of a band than as a solo artist. But even if Mel C were to be persuaded back into the recording studio, it is hard to see where they could go next. They've won, they've conquered the world – but their fans have grown up now and they no longer have the fresh-faced appeal they did just a few years ago. Perhaps the Spice Girls will turn into Spice Women, but they'll need a radical overhaul, both musically and image wise and there seems to be no impetus from anyone to get around to that.

Of course, David's future will have an enormous impact on Victoria's next move and it is still a possibility that he could play for a team in Spain or Italy. Victoria has said recently that despite her own fraught relationship with Sir Alex Ferguson, she has always encouraged David to stay with Manchester United, but Sir Alex will be retiring in May 2002. David, who is worth £25 million on the transfer market, might well decide that this is the time to make a change, and whatever she says, one can't help but suspect the sunny climate of southern Europe (to say nothing of its shopping facilities) might appeal to Victoria more than the north-west of England.

"Victoria says he has won everything at Old Trafford and wants a change," says Noel. "He is seeking new challenges and thinks playing abroad will benefit his career. Victoria says David did not sound too happy about staying long-term at Manchester United. He loves being part of the team. He loves winning and playing in front of the fans who are devoted to him but at the end of the day, feels a bit, 'Been there, done that.' He probably wouldn't go to another Premiership club, but she would up-sticks and go with him if it was abroad. Louise told me Spain was high on his list of possible targets and Victoria would be happy living there. David can have the pick of any club in the world that he wants and he will make the final decision with Victoria. She will go anywhere with him so they will never be without each other."

That is almost certainly the case. David and Victoria have been joined at the hip almost from the first moment they met, sometimes referring to themselves as different sides of the

same coin. The Posh and Becks show looks set
to run for the foreseeable future, all the more so
if there are more offspring waiting in the wings.
But Victoria might have to accept a change in
the balance of their relationship. When they
first met, she was the wealthier and the more
famous of the two, and she probably still has
more money than he does, being responsible for
£18 million of their £30-million fortune.

Victoria, however, might be nearing the end
of her career, unless she pulls out all the stops
and makes some progress in the field of acting.
This is not the case with David. If he's lucky, he
might have nearly a decade more on the football
pitch, and after that can look forward to some
kind of commentary work in association with
the beautiful game. He may well become the
main breadwinner and it is difficult to see how
Victoria, so ambitious, so focused and so
determined throughout her life until now could
possibly be happy with that.

Still, you really never know. About a decade
ago, Madonna looked as if she was on the verge
of career wipe-out: she'd finally gone too far

with her book *Sex* and had appeared in some truly awful movies, including one in which it was established that she was able to give a man a pleasure-induced heart attack through the sheer force of her sexual persona. The public had seen every bit of Madonna that there was to see and they were bored. Sometimes it is better not to reveal too much.

Madonna realised this and, like the old pro she is, backed temporarily out of the limelight, got herself the lead role in *Evita*, released one of her best albums in years in the form of *Music*, and now appears to be on the verge of becoming a huntin', shootin' and fishin' matriarch. It's hard to imagine Madonna getting her kit off these days. She's a respectable married woman, for goodness sakes, with two children to think of.

Victoria may not quite have Madonna's talent for reinvention and neither, other than on the topics of plastic surgery and eating disorders, has she ignited controversy in the way Madonna has. But it's early days. Victoria is only 27 and given the absolute dedication with which she became a star, you can't help but suspect she might have a new trick up her sleeve. Even if she went away for a few years to have several more children and recover from the whirlwind that has comprised the last decade, she could still come back in her early thirties and start all over again.

As to what her fellow Spices will make of that – well, time will tell. Yet another Spice rumour surfaced recently involving three of the girls, but this time it is Victoria who is the odd one out. Reports have surfaced suggesting that Mel B, Mel C and Emma are planning a reunion but will not be asking Victoria – jealous, it is suggested, of her high profile. It would seem then, that Victoria Beckham, a woman who has been ruthless throughout her career, has finally outgrown the band who made her what she is. And who will she outgrow next?